D1829207

Random Facts

1,869 Facts to Make You Want to Learn More

Nazar Shevchenko

Copyright © 2017 by Nazar Shevchenko

All rights reserved. This book or any portion thereof may not be reproduced or used in any manner whatsoever without the express written permission of the publisher except for the use of brief quotations in a book review.

ISBN-13: 978-1979301008

ISBN-10: 197930100X

1. A cluster of bananas is called a “hand”, and a single banana is called a “finger”.

2. In the Amazon rainforest, butterflies drink the tears of turtles to provide themselves with a dietary sodium.

3. The U. S. Constitution, the Bill of Rights, and the Declaration of Independence are kept in a bomb-proof safe every night.

4. Brain forgets certain memories to avoid an information overload and emotional hangovers.

5. Nomophobia is the fear of being away from your cell phone.

6. Before WWI most deaths in the war were caused by diseases, but during WWI two thirds were killed in the battle.

7. The reason why the ice cubes look white is because of oxygen and other impurities; if the water is boiled before freezing, the ice will look clear.

8. According to scientists, the smell of newborn babies excites women in the same way an addict craving for drugs enjoys his fix.

9. Lego does not make military-themed sets because the creator didn’t want to make war seem like a child’s play.

10. During the first two years of a child’s life, parents will miss out about 6 months’ worth of sleep.

11. The difference between a graveyard and a cemetery is that a graveyard adjoins a church, whereas a cemetery does not; you can also bury ashes in a cemetery.

12. The modern toilet was invented by Thomas Crapper, hence the phrase "to take a crapper".

13. Germans were the first ones to use flamethrowers in World War I.

14. There is a fish that can walk out from water, breathe oxygen, and even walk for a short distance. It is known as the Climbing gourami.

15. There is an upside-down traffic signal in Syracuse, New York because the local Irish kids didn't want the British red above the Irish green.

16. Roughly one percent of the world's population is served by McDonald's every day.

17. Mixina is a giant worm that has teeth on its tongue.

18. There could be as many as 7,184 people in the world like you.

19. Your body cells have 23 pairs of chromosomes. Chromosome 1 is considered the largest molecule in your entire body and it is made up of 10 billion atoms. Smaller molecules such as water are made up of only 3 atoms.

20. The oldest chewing gum is 9,000 years old.

21. Mike Ilitch, the founder of Little Caesars pizza, paid Rosa Parks' rent for over 10 years until she died.

22. Bonzai diving is a sport where people throw a parachute out of the airplane and jump to get it.

23. People who have a bilingual brain are generally more efficient and can ignore distractions.

24. There is a castle in Scotland shaped like a pineapple.

25. Thomas Jefferson was afraid of public speaking.

26. To supply NFL with leather for one year it takes about 3,000 cows.

27. It turns out that humans have just as much body hair as the chimpanzees, except our hair has less use and is very fine.

28. You are born with 300 bones, but as you grow, many of them fuse and you end up with just 206.

29. Of all the scientists that have ever lived, 90 percent are still alive.

30. Earth travels 1000 miles in one minute.

31. You have more body hair in areas where you sweat the most. It has been suggested that the purpose of body hair is to store toxins that come out with sweat. Sticking toxins to the hair prevents re-absorption of the toxins by the skin so you can wash it off the next time you take a shower.

32. Coconuts kill about 150 people per year.

33. The first prototype tank was "Little Willie" designed in 1915. It carried a crew of three people and traveled at a speed of 3 mph (4.8 km/h).

34. More people are killed by cows than by sharks.

35. There are enough toxins in The Golden Poison Dart Frog's skin to kill 100 people.

36. Avocadoes can poison birds.

37. The weight of a hummingbird is less than a penny.

38. The reason why dogs lift their leg high while urinating is because they want to leave a mark higher, so it creates an impression that they are tall and intimidating.

39. People are most allergic to milk than any other food.

40. The fear of fun is known as Cherophobia.

41. A "false memory" is when your brain thinks that something happened when in reality it didn't.

42. There are pills that can make your farts smell like roses and chocolate.

43. A dog can understand up to 250 words and gestures.

44. In ancient Babylon, a bartender would be executed if he watered down beer.

45. A mole can dig a 300 feet long tunnel in just one night.

46. Birds do no urinate.

47. More than 1,000 planets have been found in the past 20 years.

48. A human body has 60,000 miles of blood vessels.

49. When a pregnant woman has an organ damage, a baby in her womb sends stem cells to repair the damage.

50. You would be nicknamed a "heavy user" by McDonald's if you stop there frequently.

51. An owl cannot digest fur, feathers, and claws. The owl throws it up after few hours of eating.

52. Real diamonds do not show up on X-rays.

53. It costs an average of $245,000 USD to raise a child before college in the US.

54. Your thigh bones are stronger than concrete.

55. "Colgate" toothpaste translates as "Go hang yourself" in Spanish.

56. Coconut water is very similar to the blood plasma.

57. The first country in the world that adopted daylight saving time in 1916 (during the war) was Germany.

58. Bitcoin was founded by a man called Satoshi Nakamoto. His real name and who he is are not known. He has about 1 million bitcoins, equivalent to $1.1 billion.

59. During WWI, artillery barrage and mines created an immense noise. An explosion in Belgium could be heard in London 140 miles away (220 km).

60. Some butterflies travel as far as 3,000 miles.

61. During World War II, prisoners in Canadian war camps were treated so well that they didn't want to leave.

62. Mountain lions can whistle.

63. In the United States 200,000-400,000 people die each year due to medical errors that could be prevented. Preventable medical errors are the third cause of death in the US – after heart disease and cancer as of 2017.

64. A hamster runs about 8 miles on a wheel at night.

65. The world's top cause of death is heart disease which is responsible for 35% of the death cases on earth.

66. Southern sea otters have pockets in their skin that they use to store food and stones when diving.

67. Japanese Kamikaze pilots could return if they didn't find a suitable target. One pilot was shot after his ninth return.

68. When a gorilla is happy it burps.

69. To make it hard for telemarketers to pronounce his name, a British man changed his name to Tim Pppppppppprice.

70. Ancient Greeks thought that wearing pants was "ridiculous" and the Romans thought it was uncivilized. Only Barbarians wore the pants.

71. An Indian Cobra can spit poison exactly into the eye of its prey from 2.4 meters.

72. Nikola Tesla and Mark Twain were best friends.

73. Female plant lice are born pregnant.

74. James Buchanan was the fifteenth president of the US who continuously bought slaves to free them.

75. Every fifth person believes that there are aliens on our planet disguised as humans.

76. The price of a movie ticket in Tokyo is more expensive than in Mexico by 26 times.

77. The human brain is almost the size of a pillowcase if you spread it out.

78. About 30 percent of Titanic's crew and passengers survived.

79. Muhammad Ali was banned from boxing for 3 years, stripped off his title and sentenced to a 5 year prison term for refusing to serve in the US army.

80. Salt was as valuable as gold in Roman times and soldiers were sometimes paid in salt, hence the word 'salary'.

81. Crooked teeth are considered attractive in Japan.

82. A woman in Sweden lost her wedding ring; she was able to find it 16 years later on a growing carrot in her garden.

83. If a sumo makes your baby cry it is considered a good luck in Japan.

84. In one bed there can be as many as six billion dust mites.

85. Sunandha Kumariratana, Thailand's queen, drowned in 1880 as her servants watched because they were forbidden to touch her.

86. Tree-dwelling pygmy marmoset are the smallest monkeys on earth. The most that they can reach is 6 ounces in weight and 5 inches in length.

87. The mosquito repellants do not repel the mosquitos but hide you from them by blocking their receptors, so the mosquito doesn't know where you are.

88. In developing countries people don't spend less money on food; on the contrary, poor people are known to use 60-80% of their income to purchase food.

89. Smoking rates are almost 10% higher in men than in women throughout the world.

90. Grains amount to 45% of the world's diet.

91. Over 14 million young women become mothers every year.

92. More than 80 percent of hacked computers are related to simple passwords.

93. An engine of Boeing 777 has twice the horsepower of all the Titanic's steam engines combined.

94. Women are much more prone to opioids overdose than men, as they experience more chronic pain, they are more sensitive to it and tend to take prescription opioids for a longer period than men do. 48,000 women in the United States died because of such overdose between 1999 and 2010.

95. 85 percent of bikinis sold never touch the water.

96. Keanu Reeves distributed his Matrix Movies salary (around $80 million) among the special effects and makeup team for their hard work on the movie.

97. There are 54 bones in the human hand.

98. The most popular website among people aged 35 to 44 is Alka-Seltzer.com

99. In adults the arms are the most commonly broken bones whereas in children it's the collarbone.

100. Prince Charles passionately collects toilet seats.

101. In relation to the body, the human brain is the largest brain compared to all other vertebrates.

102. Charlie Sheen pays over $100,000 per month in child support.

103. Eating dairy may lead you to have acne.

104. An orange juice bought from the store is 100 percent artificially flavored.

105. There are a total of 1665 steps in the Eiffel Tower.

106. In 2012, Singapore, a country of over 5 million people, experienced 80 days in which no robberies or thefts were reported.

107. Hitmonlee, a popular Pokemon, is based on Bruce Lee.

108. Birds do not have the ability to urinate

109. The blue Twitter bird is named Larry.

110. Earth is known to have lost 40% of its wildlife in the last 40-50 years due to industrial, urban, and technological development.

111. Our nose can discern 500,000 different smells and scents and helps us remember them in connection with our brain.

112. The country with the most diverse and numerous types of bread is Germany; there are 300 types of bread available in German culture, and it is not considered to be only an addition to main dishes, but valuable in its own way.

113. Wild parrots name their children, and that name sticks for life.

114. The industry of agriculture provides jobs for 40% of the world's population.

115. People's eyes are capable of distinguishing about 10 million different colors.

116. Los Angeles was originally named El Pueblo de Nuestra Señora la Reina de **los** Ángeles del Río de Porciúncula.

117. If a lion and a polar bear were to fight, the polar bear would win.

118. We crave foods that have more calories because, in the distant past, food was mostly fruits and it was the most caloric food available.

119. On average, a cow releases about 400 liters of methane per day.

120. Each brain hemisphere controls an opposite side of the body.

121. Most of the Irish and Britons can trace their roots to Iraq and Syria.

122. The largest predators in the world are the polar bears.

123. Wisdom teeth are considered vestigial structures that humans inherited from herbivore ancestors that needed extra molar teeth for chewing, but in ⅓ of all people they come out sideways and are needed to be removed.

124. In America, food waste amounts to approximately 165 billion dollars every year, which represents four times the quantity of food Africa imports per year.

125. The most expensive Apple store is located on Fifth Avenue, Manhattan, New York. Its creation required over 10 million dollars and nowadays it is one of the top landmarks in technology and retail business.

126. Uber is the biggest taxi company in the world, even though it doesn't own any cars, but relies on software tools.

127. Kids who try to act cool in early adolescence are more likely to have issues with drugs and alcohol later in life.

128. A cow has four stomachs.

129. McDonald's sells 75 hamburgers every second all over the world.

130. Over one third of adult people in the United States and about 16% of children are obese.

131. The most shoplifted book in the world is the Bible.

132. The Amazon river is free of any bridges.

133. Baked beans are stewed, and not baked.

134. Walmart's most popular item is bananas.

135. Mars has blue sunsets.

136. The average lifespan of a person is currently 80 years and it is thought to increase by 3 months per year.

137. During a “Dancing Epidemic” in 1518 in Strasbourg, 400 people danced uncontrollably for one month and died of heart attack.

138. Cucumber is one of the most hydrating and refreshing vegetables in the world as it contains 96% water along with vitamins such as vitamin C, K, and B-group vitamins.

139. One of the most dangerous and subtle spices is nutmeg, because, if taken in large doses, it can work as a hallucinogen.

140. Daydreaming helps solve difficult problems, the more you daydream the better you are at dealing with complex situations.

141. On the average, people spend about 5 years of their life eating.

142. People in the United States spend over 190 billion dollars for fast food every year.

143. The language spoken by most people in the world is Mandarin Chinese.

144. Sea otters sleep while holding hands so that they do not get separated.

145. Both, Bin Laden and Hitler’s deaths were announced on the same date, 1st May.

146. An owl can turn its head 360 degrees.

147. More people are killed by donkeys than in a plane crash.

148. The Hulk movie's creator Jack Kirby was inspired by a woman who lifted a car to save her baby.

149. A duck, a rooster and a sheep were the first passengers to enjoy a hot air balloon flight.

150. Pirates can be seen wearing earrings because they believe doing so helps their eyesight.

151. Before becoming a dictator of Italy, Benito Mussolini worked as a school teacher and a journalist.

152. 60% of people in the world die because of chronic disease every year.

153. If you eat three plates full of food at a Chinese buffet, you will consume 3000 calories at once.

154. A shark replaces its teeth every 8 days.

155. Chocolate was once used as a currency in trade in the Mayan and Aztec cultures.

156. There are about 350 different shapes of pasta in the world and Italians claim that the shape can affect the taste of the food.

157. The eye of a giant squid is the size of a basketball.

158. Avocados can boost your serotonin levels and make you feel happy.

159. The Cyrillic alphabet used in Russia today originally came from Bulgaria.

160. English is 28 percent Latin, 28 percent French, and 25 percent Old and Middle English, Old Norse, and Dutch.

161. The first people to use ATM's were gamblers and prostitutes who didn't want to deal with tellers directly.

162. There are 50 million monkeys in India.

163. Oysters are on the top of the list of aphrodisiac food in the world (among others thanks to their very high zinc content), but few people know that, when they eat raw oysters, these "beings" are likely to be still alive.

164. There are people who only dream in black and white and they amount to 12% of the world population.

165. A scientific name for 1/100th of a second is a "jiffy".

166. People with blue eyes have a higher tolerance for alcohol.

167. More than half of the people in the world have never used a telephone.

168. Caramel was invented by the Arabs and initially it was used as a hair-removal tool for women instead of wax.

169. Every row of corn has an even number.

170. If a snail loses its eye, it grows a new one within a month.

171. An astonishing number of women have eating disorders such as anorexia, bulimia, or binge eating; men only amount to 10-15 % of the people who suffer from such disorders, but they are however less likely than women to seek medical assistance.

172. The strongest animal on the planet Earth is a Rhinoceros Beetle which can lift a weight 850 times greater than its size.

173. President James Madison was only 5 feet 4 inches tall and weighed less than 100 pounds.

174. In North America there used to be beavers the size of black bears.

175. The record for the longest interval without sleep is 11 days and it was set in 1964 by a Californian young man.

176. Cigarette lighters were invented before the match.

177. You can order beer at McDonald's in Germany.

178. Bananas are considered as berries botanically.

179. A sleepless night to a brain is like being drunk.

180. There are over 2,500 varieties of apples grown in the United States.

181. There are 22 countries that use Arabic as its official language.

182. Belarus is a neighbor of Russia and its name means White Russia.

183. The most authoritarian country in Europe is not Russia, but Belarus. Its president has been in office since 1994 and at one point in time he wanted to reunite his country with Russia. He even called himself the president of Russia, not Belarus. And he is probably the biggest supporter of resurrecting the Soviet Union.

184. In the Cold War, CIA agents used to communicate with one another based on their tied shoelaces

185. 15% of the people in the world are thought to be sleepwalkers.

186. Water represents 50-70% of the weight of our bodies.

187. People who smoke marijuana have an appetite that is 40% higher than that of a non-smoker.

188. Samurai would sometimes attack civilians at night to test out their sword's effectiveness.

189. A human being is known to eat about 35 tons of food throughout their entire life.

190. A common person is considered to have drunk more than 12,000 gallons of water by the time they are in their 70s.

191. In the United States, more than 50% of first marriages are likely to end, about 67% of second marriages can lead to divorce and 74-75% of third marriages are similarly not successful.

192. Japan's melody roads are roads in Japan that play music when the car is driven at the correct speed.

193. The first ever motion picture was invented by Louis Le Prince in 1888 but he mysteriously disappeared in 1890 and Edison tried to take credit for his invention.

194. The lowest marriage rate in the United States can be found in Washington D.C.

195. There are flowers in every color we could think of on earth except for black; the darkest flowers are deep and dark hues of red, burgundy, or purple.

196. The largest internal organ in our bodies is the liver which is also one capable of significant self-regeneration.

197. Interracial marriage has been legal in the United States since 1967. Such marriages were documented to represent 14-15% of all first marriages in America in the year 2008.

198. Only people are known to produce tears for emotional reasons.

199. Most people are thought to walk an average of 100,000 miles throughout their lives.

200. Once we reach adulthood, 25 % of our bones are in our feet.

201. By the time people reach the age of 60, their taste buds are reduced to almost a half of the number they had when they were younger.

202. The geographic coordinates of the great pyramid of Giza (29.9792458-N). and the value of the speed of light in vacuum (299, 792, 458), are coincidentally very similar.

203. According to the comics, Spider Man lived at 20 Ingram Street in Forest Hills, Queens. This address exists in the real world, and the family living in the house are Parkers.

204. Even though our planet has been proven to be round and not flat, it is believed that our universe is flat, and not round.

205. According to a 2017 study, the more time you spend on Facebook, the worse you feel about yourself.

206. When a star dies, it explodes releasing more energy than our sun burns in its entire existence.

207. Gamma rays released from exploding stars can cause a mass extinction on planet Earth if it reaches our planet.

208. During prohibition, people used to get prescriptions for 'medical' wine and alcohol, just like today with weed.

209. Non-verbal language amounts for much more communication than people might suspect; words only represent 7% of what we convey, paraverbal language (voice, tone, pitch, intonation etc.) amounts to 38% of our communication and body language is responsible for over 50% of what we "say".

210. Hebrew died out in 200 CE and wasn't spoken again until 13 October 1881 when a man called Eliezer Ben-

Yehuda and his friends agreed to exclusively speak Hebrew in their conversations to revive it.

211. So far people have explored only about 5% of the oceanic surface on earth.

212. It is a well-known fact that water deprivation can quickly lead to death, not lack of food; the average human being could survive without food 1-2 months, depending on their body weight, amount of fat, health condition, immunity, age etc.

213. The first same-sex marriage in the world history was surprisingly not the one that took place in Denmark in 1989 after same-sex marriage was legalized. The first same-sex marriage took place in Ancient Rome before Christianity became the official religion.

214. There seems to be a correlation between intelligence and the levels of specific minerals in our hair e.g. zinc and copper: the higher your IQ, the higher these two values in your hair.

215. According to a study, mothers of twins have longer, healthier lives.

216. Up to 50 percent of the matter in our galaxy was brought from other galaxies in the form of stardust from exploding stars. This phenomenon is known as an intergalactic wind.

217. Canada is the second largest country in the world, after Russia.

218. More than half of Russia is Siberia.

219. To buy 2 pizzas a man paid 10,000 bitcoins in 2010. Many years later it's worth 10 million dollars.

220. The most democratic country in the world is considered Norway.

221. The largest democratic country in the world is India.

222. The first democracy is ancient Greece.

223. You have more bones in your hand than anywhere else.

224. The parliament of Iceland is the longest in use and it was created in 930 by the Vikings.

225. Police investigators spent years chasing the "Phantom of Heilbronn" a female serial killer whose DNA was found at dozens of crime scenes. Investigators finally discovered that the DNA belonged to a factory worker who made the cotton swabs used to collect DNA samples.

226. Montpelier, Vermont is the only United States capital without a McDonalds.

227. The term "third world country" has nothing to do with poverty but refers to countries that, after World War II, did not align themselves with either US or the Soviet Union.

228. The King's School in Canterbury, England, is the oldest operating school in the world. It was founded in AD 597 during the Late Antiquity era, 100 years after the fall of Rome.

229. Our height might differ with almost 1 cm throughout the day, namely we are known to be slightly taller in the morning than in the evening.

230. Our planet is the only one in the whole solar system which hasn't received the name of a mythological figure.

231. The risk of heart attack is generally 20% higher in the beginning of the week, because people can be more "wound up" from weekend entertainment as well as more stressed out by the newly starting timetable at work.

232. About 90% of the diseases acknowledged in medicine are thought to be caused or complicated by a "simple" factor like stress.

233. Our breath is a strange self-regulating mechanism with a propensity for balance: we always inhale more air through one nostril when we breathe normally through our nose; moreover, one nostril takes on the "major" role every 15 minutes.

234. Did you think that Christopher Columbus was the first European to discover America? The earliest European explorers of America were the Vikings led by Leif Erickson around 1000 AD.

235. The Hundred Years' War lasted for 116 years.

236. Pigtailed macaques are trained to harvest coconuts in Thailand. Humans can only harvest 80 coconuts per day whereas the male macaques can harvest 1,600 coconuts in one day.

237. The Eiffel Tower was used by the military as a radio tower to intercept crucial military transmissions during the World War II.

238. Rwandan government has the most women as parliamentarians in the world.

239. The poorest country in the world is the Central African Republic with salaries smaller than $1000 per year.

240. The poorest city in the United States is Detroit; more than half of its population makes less than $25,000 a year.

241. McDonald's is the largest employer in Brazil.

242. The median income in the United States is about $51,000 per year.

243. Some Republicans wanted to change the name of French Fries to Liberty Fries when France refused to join the US coalition in the Iraq war.

244. Some French cafes charge extra to rude customers so that they could keep the environment arrogant-free.

245. There is so much gold hidden in the bottom of our planet, that, if people managed to extract it all from every hidden source and corner, it could cover the Earth in a layer that would amount to over 30 cm.

246. Could mosquitoes suck all the blood in a human body in a "sip"? Yes, but it would take at least 1,200,000 of such small insects to achieve that.

247. Your skin contains more life forms (albeit microscopic…) than the number of people existing on our planet.

248. In 1986 a beer drinking goat was elected as a mayor of a small town in Texas, USA.

249. Every continent has a city named Rome.

250. If there is one place in Europe that attracts the most tourists of all ages, that's Disneyland.

251. Any material can be transformed into glass if you melt it; you must only make sure you cool off the given molten "stuff" before its molecules have time to realign into the same configuration they had before melting.

252. In Tokyo, a restaurant called "The Restaurant of Order Mistakes" has hired waiters who are suffering from dementia so that they bring different orders to customers every time for the element of surprise.

253. When you cry out for help and call out specific people, like the guy in a green shirt, it makes them more likely to act.

254. According to scientists, sunflowers can clean up the radioactive contamination from the soil and reduce pollution.

255. SADS, Sudden Arrhythmic Death Syndrome, is a condition where an adult dies suddenly during a sleep.

256. Multitasking was a cup of tea for Leonardo da Vinci. Could he draw several paintings at the same time with only two hands? No, but what he could do is nonetheless amazing enough: he is known to be able to simultaneously draw with one hand and write with the other.

257. If you thought the chameleon or the skin-shedding snake are the most spectacular creatures on earth, you probably haven't heard of the mimic octopus which changes not only its colors, but also its shape as in a "mimicry" of other animals (especially sea animals like the lionfish or sea snakes).

258. Uranus was discovered before Antarctica.

259. The place with the largest number of Döner Kebabs is not Istanbul, as you may think, but the capital of Germany and multiculturalism, Berlin.

260. The number of people on earth who live in regions where it never snows amounts to 2/3 of the whole earth's population.

261. Did you think you need to earn a million dollars to fall into the top one percent in the US? In the United States you need to earn at least $389,436 per year to be considered as a top one percent.

262. New York city is the most populated city in the United States with over 8 million residents.

263. Tokyo, Japan is the most populated city in the world with over 37 million people.

264. Kim Peek was an American, known for his extraordinary memory and his ability to read two pages of a book simultaneously with each eye.

265. If you want to eat dried fruit, keep in mind that such a process reduces their vitamin and antioxidant content by over 40%.

266. Ignorant people are more likely to believe that they are brilliant whereas intelligent people are more likely to underestimate their abilities.

267. Most of us walk so much in our lifetime, that the distance could be as long as three times the whole surface of the earth.

268. In a country made of many islands as Greece is, 40% of the inhabitants live in the capital, Athens.

269. Ikea is one of the most preferred "brands" for beds in Europe: 10% of the children on this continent are conceived in such a piece of furniture.

270. The United States has invaded Canada twice, in 1775 and in 1812.

271. A box jellyfish can kill a human in under 120 seconds with its poison.

272. Rwanda is said to be the most litter-free state in Africa as plastic bags are illegal to carry in Rwanda and they can charge you a fine of $100-$150.

273. Prisoners in California are housed at the cost of $75,560 which is surprisingly more than the cost of a year at Harvard.

274. Onagadori is a type of chicken breed found in Japan with tails as high as 27 feet.

275. During the filming of The Dark Knight, Michael Caine forgot his lines as he was terrified of Heath Ledger in his joker Makeup.

276. Chocolate originated in the Americas and was introduced to the Europeans by the Aztecs.

277. According to research, the internet makes your brain lazy.

278. A famous British admiral Horatio Nelson suffered from seasickness his whole life.

279. The first blood transfusion was done in 1667 after which the patient got better.

280. It is well known that trees have very long lives. The oldest tree in the world is 4,845 years old and it is in California.

281. Scotland has about the same land area as the state of Maine, Czech Republic, and United Arab Emirates. But it always seemed so big on the map!

282. Mount Everest is the tallest mountain in the world and it was named after a Welshman Sir George Everest.

283. The Pineberry is a white strawberry that tastes like a pineapple.

284. A very large part of Russia is uninhabited; over 13,000 of its villages have no inhabitants at this point in time.

285. Kazakhstan is the origin of all the apples; 90 percent of modern apples can be traced back to 2 trees.

286. Ming the Clam, the world's oldest animal at 507, was killed by researchers trying to find out how old it was.

287. On average a chicken produces 190 eggs per year.

288. The first magazine in the world history was published in Germany in 1663.

289. A baby's head amounts to ¼ of its bodily surface, but by the age of 25 this part is only 1/8 of our bodies.

290. The only dog whose tongue is not pink is Chau-Chau.

291. Can you chew and lose weight? With the "chewing gum strategy" – you can. It is a proven fact that we can burn 10-11 calories per hour if we chew gum.

292. Have you ever wondered how much time of your life you spend waiting at the street lights for a green light? The average person spends about six months overall if they strictly respect traffic rules.

293. A goldfish has a memory of 3 seconds.

294. The oldest known civilization in history is considered Mesopotamia, modern day Iraq. It was so old that even the ancient Greeks referred to it as ancient history.

295. Gunpowder was invented by Chinese alchemists by accident. They were trying to make a potion of immortality but instead found a way to make an explosion.

296. Genghis Khan was the founder of the Mongol Empire, the largest empire of its time. It is believed that up to 16 million individuals alive today are direct descendants of the Mongol leader.

297. Our memory is not only affected by factors such as age, diet, minerals and vitamins, brain training etc. Science shows that a simple thing like posture can influence our memory centers and trigger specific memories.

298. If you thought the distance from New York to London is always the same, you might want to consider the fact that the American city drifts about one inch away from the British capital every year.

299. Of all the animals in the world only a human and a dog have a prostate.

300. A common souvenir for tourists to bring home from the US is a Red Solo cup.

301. King George V of England had a dragon tattoo on his arm.

302. Tesla is now worth more than Ford Motor Company.

303. "Fart Proudly" was a scientific essay about farts written by Benjamin Franklin.

304. In the past 10+ years, more than 10,000 trees have been planted by two disabled men in China. One without arms and the other without sight.

305. If they didn't put a dye into Coca-Cola, it would be green.

306. Nestle was formed because of two competing milk companies merging.

307. In the United States, over 500,000 animals are killed every hour to produce edible meat and related food.

308. At a very young age, twins can develop their own language that they can use to communicate with each other and that nobody else understands.

309. Did you think that worms might feed on earth if they don't find any available food? They are known to start eating themselves.

310. There are more insects per square kilometer than humans in the world.

311. Have you ever wondered why babies seem to have large eyes? The answer is rooted in an anatomical fact: while our nose and ears keep changing and growing as we become adults, our eyes stay the same size they have when we are born.

312. Whales evolved from land animals.

313. The smartest breed of a dog in the world is a Border Collie.

314. All vertebrates from fish to humans have one thing in common, they all have a spine. Life could have originated in the water.

315. Worms taste like fried bacon.

316. The reintroduction of wolves to the Yellowstone in 1995 lead to regrowth of many populations and even saved the rivers from erosion.

317. The inconclusive ending of World War I led to World War II.

318. One Russian scientist was able to breed a pet fox.

319. Foxes mostly hunt on their own instead of packs like in wolves.

320. A chicken can fly for 13 seconds at most.

321. During the 19th century, committing suicide was considered a serious crime and the culprit was ordered to be hanged if he survived the suicide.

322. A notable useful property of a giraffe's tongue (usually over 20-inch long) is the fact that it can be used to clean the animal's ears.

323. Being left-handed can be dangerous: over 2,500 left-handed people per year die because of misuse of tools and devices made for right-handed persons.

324. Many of our cells can benefit from a degree of regeneration (and consequently our organs) except for our teeth which can only use the repair abilities of a dentist.

325. It takes more energy to digest foods such as celery, cabbage, and apples, than the amount gained from eating them.

326. Donald the Duck is banned from the public scene in Finland because the duck doesn't wear any pants.

327. A cat in Texas, called Dusty, gave birth to 420 kittens throughout her life in a span of 17 years.

328. In 1830s ketchup was used in medicine.

329. If you try to stop a sneeze you can possibly damage your diaphragm, your eyes and your eardrums.

330. Ronald Wayne, former Apple co-founder, sold his 10% stakes for $800 due to issues with Steve Jobs. This would've been worth $35 billion today.

331. During harsh weathers, snails can hibernate to survive and go to sleep for 3 years straight.

332. In the United Nations there are six official languages" English, French, Arabic, Chinese, Spanish, and Russian.

333. The idea that Ancient Egyptians used slaves to build pyramids is now dismissed as a myth. This idea was proposed by a Greek historian Herodotus in fifth century B.C., but there is enough evidence to show that the work was done by paid laborers.

334. Men and women in Egypt used to wear makeup, which they believed gave them protection of gods Horus and Ra.

335. Lobsters have a blue blood.

336. Insects have a yellow blood.

337. Nowadays it is hard to find a person who doesn't know how to read or write, but in ancient times, less than 10 percent of people were literate.

338. One of Joseph Stalin's children, Svetlana, defected to the United States in 1967. She lived happily in the US for the rest of her life and died in 2011.

339. If cryonics is still ambiguous and largely unreliable as a branch of medical science, since there is no proof that frozen human bodies could ever return to life, nature may surprise us with a strange fact: frozen lobsters are known to return to life when thawed.

340. The so-called "Africanized bee" is one of the most dangerous beings on earth. It was born out of the interbreeding effort of a beekeeper in Brazil whose experiment failed. It is a hybrid of European and African bee species and it has become feared on the American continent because it swarms excessively, and it can chase its targets for a very long time and distance.

341. Bearded men are more trusted than clean-shaven.

342. Everyday 12 babies in hospitals are given to the wrong parents.

343. In 1945 the British started designing tanks with tea-making equipment.

344. How many people does it take to circle the earth around the Equator? It's enough to have 33 million people holding hands.

345. In New York there is a law that forbids selling a house that is haunted without informing the potential buyers about this fact.

346. France holds the record for having the maximum number of time zones which is 12, while America and Russia have 11 time zones.

347. The female lions bring 90 percent of all the prey.

348. The heart of a hedgehog beats 300 times per minute.

349. After leaking NSA secrets, Edward Snowden was refused asylum by the UK, China and many other countries until Russia took him in.

350. There's a mountain on Mars named 'Olympus Mons' which is three times the height of Mt. Everest and is the tallest mountain seen by a man.

351. Eugene Cernan was the last Apollo to journey to the moon on his daughter's request, which was to carve her initials. 'TDC', on the moon, which he did.

352. A steady stream of minor accomplishments makes you more satisfied with your life than a few major accomplishments.

353. In 1960's, The CIA implanted batteries, microphones and listening devices to spy on Kremlin and the Russians. The program was referred to as "Acoustic Kitty'.

354. There were six American presidents who were left handed. Obama was the sixth.

355. J.K. Rowling was offered to play the role of Harry Potter's mother, but she turned it down.

356. The money is made not from paper, but from cotton.

357. Los Angeles is ¼ cars. How come? About a quarter of its land surface is regularly covered by cars (whether parked, or in motion).

358. Mosquitoes kill more people than any other creatures combined.

359. If you go to a casino in Las Vegas, you are prone to lose the sense of time, as there are no clocks in such places. The reason may have to do with the fact that everything is supposed to move "gambling wheel-wise" in Las Vegas.

360. Germany has the highest number of football fan clubs in the world.

361. Why was the dangerous cone snail called a cigarette snail? It's not because it can reach a long, thin shape, or because it can be as fatal as tobacco. The name is rooted in the fact that, once stung by this rare and strange creature, you will only have enough time to live to smoke a whole cigarette.

362. Mandarin Chinese is the hardest language to learn for an English speaker.

363. An eye contact between a man and a woman in Afghanistan is not acceptable.

364. The capital of Liberia, Monrovia, is named after an American president James Monroe.

365. Andrew Jackson taught his parrot how to swear and curse.

366. The only president to never marry was James Buchanan.

367. The longest traffic car jam in the world occurred in Beijing, China, in the year 2010 which lasted for 12 days.

368. There is a village in Netherlands that is named Giethoorn which has no roads and is connected by foot bridges and canals.

369. The approximate time it will take to watch every video on YouTube is a thousand years.

370. Before the rise of colonialism, Africa used to have 10,000 different states and culturally independent groups which had different languages and traditions.

371. Have you ever looked an ostrich in its eye? You might want to, because strangely enough this bird's eye is bigger than its brain.

372. Did you think that only snakes shed skin? Humans do something similar, too. We are known to shed 40 pounds of skin throughout our lives, as our skin replaces itself to a certain extent on a regular basis.

373. China forbade TV programs referring to time travel because of the illusion of history and meaning such content creates. A national regulatory authority banned all time travel content from public view, preferring to focus on typically Chinese artistic/media production instead.

374. Does sleep help you burn calories? It might happen especially if you choose a cold room. In any case, sleep is proven to burn more calories than sitting on a couch or in an armchair and watching TV (no matter how few they may be).

375. A starfish can regenerate itself through its arms. If one arm starts to grow again, it can help the whole body of this creature to regenerate.

376. Clouds don't only weigh as a gloomy burden on our shoulders; they have real physical weight. A cloud can amount even to one million pounds.

377. Germany is one of the countries with the highest population density in the world – do Germans just organize their space to the maximum or is it because of their immigrant-friendly mentality?

378. The English language is widely-known as the language with the highest amount of words in the world. But how many of us know which English word has the largest number of meanings? The verb "set" comes first and it is followed by "run".

379. An American citizen Charles Osborn had hiccups for around 68 years and is listed in the Guinness Book of World Records.

380. It takes over 3,000 folding attempts in the same place before an American dollar banknote can be torn apart. Does such a fact perhaps increase the worth of this currency …?

381. The highest court in the US is a baseball court. Why is it so well-placed on top of its surroundings? It's because it is located above the Supreme Court.

382. There are sometimes many deliberations regarding the public "face" of Facebook. Did you know that the "Like" button could have actually been called "Awesome"? Now isn't that a notable difference for the value of the content many people post on this social network!

383. If you thought people only read the Bible in printed form (possibly in a pious posture next to their bed or in front of a religious icon), you were quite wrong. The Bible is one of the top 3 bestsellers on Amazon-Kindle, together with the biography of Steve Jobs and the Hunger Games.

384. Coyotes have incredibly keen sense of hearing: they can know when a mouse is nearby even if it moves beneath a very thick stratum of snow.

385. Woodrow Wilson was the only president to have a PhD degree. It was in political science and history.

386. By 2050, Africa's population is expected to get doubled and reach 2.3 billion.

387. A pig was hanged in France before the public in 1938 for killing a child.

388. A tapeworm was found in a human body which was about 33 meters in length, making it the longest tapeworm in history.

389. In Japan, some industries allow employees to sleep while at work.

390. At least one American is living in North Korea right now voluntarily.

391. The world population is growing by about 85 million people a year.

392. The least populated country in the world is Vatican City with only about 451 people.

393. Greenland has been populated by the people from Canada and Nordic countries for over 4500 years.

394. A camel can survive two weeks without water.

395. Greenland is the least populated territory in the world with less than 0.03 people per square kilometer.

396. Greece has a hard time building a subway system because they keep digging up ancient ruins.

397. Is Greenland a country? It is a territory owned by Denmark.

398. Caracas, Venezuela holds the record of having the highest crime rate in the world.

399. Tanzanite stone is said to be 1000x rarer than diamond as it can only be found in one place in the entire world, foothills of Mount Kilimanjaro, Tanzania.

400. The most aged living Hollywood actor till date is Norman Lloyd who is cast in a show which is to be released in 2018.

401. Isabella Stewart Gardner Museum in Boston holds the record of arranging the wealthiest art heist till date, it held 13 paintings worth $500 million.

402. It takes 75,000 flowers to extract a single pound of the saffron spice.

403. Netherlands and Belgium are the most densely populated countries in Europe with about 394 and 344 people per square kilometer.

404. A giraffe can go without water longer than a camel.

405. Rats can go without water longer than anyone else.

406. A kangaroo rat can go without water completely, it gets its water from its meagre diet.

407. While United States borders only 2 countries, Russia borders 14.

408. The hippopotamus has enough room between its teeth for a child: if it opens its mouth wide enough, it could suit a kid whose height is a couple of feet.

409. How much do bacteria generally weigh? More than you think and a (small) part of our whole-body weight. The bacteria "hidden" in our bodies can weigh 3-8 pounds.

410. There is a small amount of anandamide, a marijuana-like chemical, in chocolate. This directly affects the brain's pleasure center.

411. Shakespeare's autograph is worth more than $5 million.

412. Men are more likely to be struck by lightning than women. Is it a matter of hormonal attraction or just more lack of carefulness about the surroundings?

413. Jose Mujica is a former President of Uruguay who is considered the poorest president in the world. He donated 90 percent of his $12,000 monthly salary to charities and would even wait his turn at public hospitals.

414. Pigs cannot move their necks and their heads enough to be able to look up at the sky.

415. In the last decade, Afghanistan was in the news more than any other country.

416. Oceans cover about 70 percent of the Earth's surface.

417. The largest ocean in the world is the Pacific and it covers 30 percent of the world.

418. Women's brains seem to be active in more areas than in men especially in the areas involved in impulse control, focus, and emotions, whereas the men's brain is more active in visual and coordination areas of the brain.

419. There is a town in Norway called "Hell" which freezes almost every winter.

420. Masseter, located in the jaw, is the strongest muscle based on its weight. When you close your teeth, masseter can exert a force as strong as 200 pounds (90.7 kilograms) on the molars.

421. Just to know why being right-handed passes for normality: statistically only 10% of the people on earth are left-handed.

422. Blueberries don't ripe until you pick them up; and then they taste as if they were still unripe!

423. According to a British study, the average office worker spends over 500 USD per year on gifts for workmates on various occasions such as birthdays and public celebrations. In a 40-year career that's about 20,000 USD overall. The same study discovered that 42% of men and 34 % women are quite dissatisfied with such expenditures of social life at work and felt pressured to contribute.

424. An experimentalist wanted to sell New Zealand on eBay in 2006 for a price that only got as high as 3000 USD until the selling ad was invalidated and shut down.

425. A bee must collect pollen from 2 million flowers in order to produce one pound of honey.

426. January is named after Janus, the Roman God of two faces, one that looks back to the past and the other that looks forward to the future.

427. Gorillas can get sick with cold.

428. Liver is the only organ that can regenerate itself.

429. The last surviving soldier of World War I died in 2011 at 110 years old. His name was Frank Buckles.

430. In Japan, death from overworking is very common.

431. The largest animal in the world is the blue whale.

432. The heaviest land animal in the world is the African Bush Elephant.

433. The last wooly mammoths died in 1650 BCE on a Wrangel Island, north of Siberia. The Great Pyramids of Giza were 1000 years old by then.

434. There are people who revived and now worship ancient Greek gods.

435. The shortest men in the world live in East Timor where an average height is 1.6 meters, or 5 ft 2 in.

436. French citizens are honored with medals by the French government on successfully bringing up their children with dignity.

437. Cold welding is a procedure that only occurs in space, it involves bonding metals together.

438. The Danish charity store Wefood sells only products that are past their sell-by date. It is in Copenhagen and in 2016 it opened its second branch because of obvious success and benefit to many people. Food is sold for half the price it would have in a supermarket and people are interested in good products, even if they are no longer theoretically "valid". The aim of such "alternative" food marketers is combating global food waste which amounts to 1.3 billion tons per year according to the UN Food and Agriculture Association.

439. Have you ever wondered how many people are flying over the US at a given point during a normal day? Since this country is so large and active from many points of view, over 50,000 people are sitting in an airplane flying over its territory this very moment.

440. A third of all the food in the world is eaten by insects.

441. Even without sitting every day in front of a feast, a regular person produces an amount of saliva in their whole life that could fill two swimming pools.

442. It's rather convenient to have a tarantula as a pet, because it can live even longer than two years without any kind of food.

443. Would you buy anything marked by the brand "Apple"? When it comes to technology – probably. But how about an after-shave lotion or a pair of sneakers? Such things are not as far away in fantasy as you may think. Apple launched a clothing line in 1986 and no wonder if this is the first time you hear such fact.

444. Aleix Segura Vendrell holds the record of holding his breath for 24 minutes and 3 seconds underwater.

445. Purple is said to be a royal color because it was difficult to extract in old times, therefore only wealthy people could afford it.

446. Two of the most famous TV shows, Friends and Game of Thrones have similar per episode budget of about $10 million.

447. Dogs see the world in black and white, nevertheless their vision is much better than human's.

448. The world's most educated country is Canada with more than half of its population with a college degree.

449. There are more lakes in Canada than in the rest of the world combined.

450. The largest coastline in the world is in Canada.

451. There are three countries in the world that have not adopted the metric system; they are the United States of America, Burma, and Liberia.

452. Qatar is the wealthiest country in the world. If you divide its wealth by the number of individuals you would get around $130,000 per person per year. Whereas the US is only about $57,000 per person.

453. Mosquito's favorite color is blue.

454. Eminem's mother filed an $11 million lawsuit on her own son for defaming her in a song but got settled for $25,000.

455. A high amount of the dust we find in our homes and we clean up so eagerly (sometimes in full disgust) is made of dead skin.

456. Unlike other beings, cockroaches can go on living for a few weeks without their heads, as their brain is located inside their body. However, they will die of hunger after a while.

457. There is a church in the Czech Republic whose fame derives mainly from the fact that its chandelier is made of human bones. Could people be drawn to no-nonsense images of death more than to imaginary afterlife?

458. The first female mayor in America was elected in 1887. She was nominated by a group of men who did it as a joke, but she still won over 60 percent of the vote.

459. The only animal that cannot jump at all is an elephant…not even when it's smaller.

460. In January 2017 a man called Robert Marchand broke a record when he cycled 22.5 km around the Saint-Quentin-en-Yvelines vélodrome near Paris. It was his age that made him famous and so worthy of admiration:

he is 105 years old and fully believes in what cycling can do for his health and longevity.

461. Sim Jae Deok was a South Korean who was born in a toilet, became a mayor and worked to improve the toilet system and turned his own home into a giant toilet shaped house. He was called "Mr. Toilet".

462. In the German Empire in 1916 it was allowed to take passport photos with your dog.

463. Femur is the largest and strongest bone in the human body; it can support 30 times the weight of one person.

464. Michael Larson, an ice cream truck driver won $110,237 in the game show called 'Press Your Luck' in a single episode by memorizing the entire game system for six consecutive weeks.

465. You can burn around 150 calories by banging your head on the wall.

466. As of 2016, there is enough proven oil reserves to meet about 50 years of global production.

467. Bats were trained to drop bombs in World War II by America.

468. A gasoline car uses only 14-26 percent of the stored chemical energy in the fuel, whereas the electric car uses up to 80 percent of its energy.

469. Germany produces more renewable energy than it can use.

470. People from Ohio are the most likely to use curse words.

471. Due to deforestation, the area of rainforests is less than half of what it used to be.

472. The largest producers of paper and paper products are the United States and Canada.

473. Cats are thought to be primarily responsible for the extinction of 33 species of birds.

474. The word robot is derived from the Czech word “robota” which means work.

475. In China, Skype is banned from being used by the public.

476. If you are under 38, the funniest joke you will ever hear in your life is a joke you haven’t heard yet.

477. There is a scientific unit used to measure the ‘risk of death’ of any action: the micromort. If the action is rated with a micromort you have a one in a million chance of dying. Running a marathon is ~7 micromorts, skydiving 10, and climbing Mount Everest 40,000.

478. King Henry III used to sleep with a huge axe by his side.

479. A flock of crows is called a murder.

480. Psychologists have accepted the addiction of Facebook to be a real mental disorder.

481. Around 50% of Uganda's population is under the age of 15.

482. The first Apple computer had a hard drive with only 5 megabytes of memory.

483. In Japan there are more electric charging stations than there are gas stations.

484. The first computer was created in 1822 by Charles Babbage.

485. Nintendo started off as a playing card company in 1889.

486. Modern smartphones such as iPhone 6 have about 600 times more transistors than 1995 Intel Pentium computers. Back then, modern smartphones would be considered supercomputers.

487. Only one Jewish person lives in Afghanistan today and his name is Zablon Simintov.

488. Only 10 percent of the world currency is physical money, the rest is in the computer.

489. The first computer mouse was invented in 1964 by Doug Engelbart and it was made of wood.

490. France produces nearly a billion tons of cheese a year in around 1,200 different varieties.

491. Bloodhounds are the only animals that can testify evidence at the court.

492. The eyes of a donkey are so weirdly (and effectively) placed, that it can see all of its feet anytime it wants.

493. In Denmark there is a list of officially approved names that parents can use for their newborn babies due to a special law meant to keep names conventional.

494. You can get goosebumps even after you die.

495. The Spanish national anthem contains zero words.

496. OJ Simpson was originally selected to play Terminator, but the studio thought he would not suit the character and was hence replaced.

497. Honey never spoils

498. 12 percent of dreamers used to dream in black and white; but this percentage decreased after the arrival of color television.

499. You have a new skeleton every 10 years.

500. Every month more than 5000 computer viruses are released.

501. The brain can hold more than 3580 terabytes of memory.

502. When you look at a computer screen you blink on average of 7 times per minute, but when you are not looking, you blink about 20 times per minute.

503. Mexicans are the largest immigrant group in the United States today.

504. The Latino population makes up about 17 percent of the total US population; Asians make up 5 percent.

505. A flee can jump and reach a height which is over 200 times higher than its own dimensions.

506. Up to 200 muscles are being used when a person makes only one step.

507. France considers post-mortem marriage something natural and desirable. Posthumous alliance has been legal for many centuries. An example of such incidents can be found in situations in which someone in a close relationship dies suddenly and the partner left behind can marry them. People only need to prove there was a marriage intention before death and have the permission of the family of the deceased.

508. A baby blue whale gains up to 250 pounds (113 kg) every day for the first year of its life.

509. The number of chopsticks used by the Chinese people on a yearly basis is 45 billion.

510. In the US, almost half of the women who give birth are not married.

511. Somebody left a note in an FBI office that said, “Please don’t lock this door tonight”. This note was left by burglars who were able to steal records from the FBI in 1971.

512. In the UK, almost 4 million workers commute for 2 hours each day, while the average duration of a commute within the general population is about 50 minutes.

513. Our tongue prints are as unique as our fingerprints.

514. Birth control pills made for humans also work on gorillas.

515. There are over 200 dead bodies of hikers buried in the Mt. Everest.

516. All the clocks shown in the movie Pulp Fiction show the same time, 4:20.

517. Beer was once classified as a soft drink in Russia.

518. Your sneeze can travel at a speed of 100 mph.

519. In 1950s the main group of immigrants to the United States came from Europe and Canada.

520. The word 'nerd' was invented by Dr. Seuss.

521. The longest freshwater coastline is in Michigan, US.

522. Fanta orange was invented because of Hitler's embargo on Coca-Cola, and it was only available in Germany for that time.

523. Volkswagen became the second largest car producer in the world during Hitler's time in power.

524. Dragonflies are the fastest flying insects. Their speed can reach 100 km per hour.

525. Ten percent of all waste generated is plastic.

526. Greenland is considered the largest island in the world.

527. The largest peninsula in the world is the Arabian Peninsula, and it has seven countries.

528. The gas lamp was invented by a Ukrainian pharmacist.

529. The smokes from a large-scale nuclear war could cause an Ice Age on Earth.

530. There are eight nuclear countries in the world with additional three countries suspccted to own nuclear weapons.

531. A jellyfish is composed of 95% water.

532. World's biggest honey bees are found in the Himalayas that measure up to 3 cm and are known to make hallucinogenic honey.

533. Your body detects taste in 0.0015 seconds which is faster than a blink of an eye.

534. Costa Rica is the 12th happiest country despite having no army.

535. In 1958, two pilots created a record of flying for two months without landing even for once.

536. Five percent of the world lives in the US but Americans consume about 37 percent of the world's cocaine.

537. 'Rolling Coal' is when some people modify their cars to produce thick black diesel smoke to protest and annoy cyclists and environmentalists.

538. During the Second World War, Clint Eastwood's plane crashed into the sea and swam 2 miles to the shore to get to safety.

539. You can fit more than a million earths in the sun.

540. There have been five mass extinctions in the history of the Earth.

541. One in every 5 people in the US die from smoking.

542. Pizza farms is a place where they grow all the ingredients to produce a pizza.

543. After three days of death, the digestive enzymes used to break down food start to break down the body.

544. The first soda pop made in the US is Vernors Ginger Ale and it was made in Detroit in 1860s.

545. 41% of the kids in Africa are involved in different forms of child labor; the ages of the children forced to work range between 5 and 14 years.

546. Research showed that 300 million people in China are obese, which makes this country one of the top states in terms of obesity, second only to the USA.

547. If there is $10 in your wallet and no debt, you're wealthier than 25 percent of Americans.

548. America is the nation with the highest number of people suffering from personality disorders.

549. Scotland's national animal (a mascot or a totem?) is the unicorn.

550. The Chernobyl disaster is said to have released 400 times more radioactive contamination than a nuclear bomb.

551. Bubbles cannot exist in space.

552. In Japan you can get multiple varieties of KitKat bars: strawberry cheesecake, green tea, sweet potato, red bean sandwich, and sake.

553. Actor Kal Penn managed to raise around $800,000 in a charity to prove a guy wrong who said Kal doesn't belong in America.

554. The founder of BMW, Gunther Quandt, was a Nazi supporter and provided the Nazis with ammunitions.

555. A man who started a site to help people find cheap flight tickets was sued by the United Airlines.

556. IP man star, Donnie Yen, hospitalized 8 out of 10 men who harassed his girlfriend at a bar in 1990.

557. Bobby Pearce, an Australian rower in 1928 Olympics, won the race despite waiting in mid-race so that a family of ducks could pass.

558. According to a study, about 60 percent of dreams are forgotten five minutes after waking up.

559. The angle of Earth's tilt oscillates between 22.1 and 24.5 degrees every 41,000 years; currently it is at 23.44.

560. Ants never sleep.

561. There was a woman who sued Walmart over 2 cents and won!

562. An average man spends nearly a year of his life simply staring at women.

563. There are more chances of getting skin cancer from tanning beds than getting lung cancer from smoking.

564. The taste of a vegetable depends on the way you cut it.

565. 4000 years ago, the Sahara Desert was covered by a forest and vegetation.

566. It costs on average between $1,500 to $3,300 a year to be a smoker.

567. Some people can wake up at the right time just by anticipating it; their body releases stress hormones an hour before waking up.

568. In U.S., second hand smoking is responsible for 50,000 deaths each year.

569. The static that you see on TV or hear on the radio is an echo of the Big Bang.

570. It takes 8 minutes for the photon of light to travel from the sun to the earth.

571. It takes 40,000 years for the photon of light to travel from the core of the sun to its surface.

572. Brian Robson was a homesick Welshman living in Australia who was too broke to get home. He decided to mail himself in a crate back to the UK nearly dying in the process, only to find himself in Los Angeles by accident.

573. Jackie Chan dubbed the lines for the Beast in the Chinese translation of Disney's animated classic Beauty and the Beast, and he also sang all the Beast's songs in Mandarin.

574. Chewing gum has been banned in Singapore since 1992, as Chinese leaders claimed it can make the streets and means of transport more dirty than necessary. Nevertheless since 2004 chewing gum can be used in dentistry and pharmacy for medical purposes.

575. UN put the cost of solving World Hunger at $30 billion a year. That's less than $100 a year or around $7 a month per person in the United States.

576. Almost 20 million Americans live in mobile homes and enjoy their road vans as a mixture of comfort, freedom, and alternative lifestyle.

577. The famous Statue of Liberty, often overused as a symbol of the US, was made in France and offered as a gift to the Americans.

578. The first woman to become a millionaire in the US was Sara Breedlove who sold hair products.

579. The Great Frigate Bird sleeps in 12 second bursts while in flight, allowing them to fly non-stop for months at a time.

580. South Dakota holds an annual motorcycle race that results in 10 deaths, 400 arrests and 300 emergency incidents on an average.

581. Despacito is now the most watched YouTube video of all time with over 3,476,567,972 views as of 2017.

582. Before the Age of Renaissance, most of the books in the world were in Chinese.

583. In 1962, a typo error (hyphen) in the code caused a rocket to explode soon after takeoff, causing NASA $630 million.

584. A quarter of medicinal plants were discovered in the rainforests.

585. More than 70 percent of medicinal plants used to treat cancer are found in the tropical rain forest.

586. Of all the plants in the tropical rainforest, less than one percent has been studied to determine their medicinal value.

587. Clicking selfies cause more injuries than shark attacks.

588. Around 10,000 toxic carrying ships lose their course of direction each year, and 10% end up leaking those toxics into the sea.

589. Around 176 million new users have signed up for social media accounts in the past year.

590. In 1923, Jockey Frank died of a heart attack during a race; however, his horse crossed the finish line with Frank on his back, declaring him the winner.

591. The total amount of distinct species found on the planet Earth is 9 million.

592. The animals that have the biggest brains on Earth are the Sperm Whales.

593. The plastic waste will take about 500 to 1000 years to break down.

594. You cannot taste salt until you are four months old because your kidneys start to process salt at about that age.

595. Indiana University received $1 Million from the US Government to study memes.

596. The number of languages spoken throughout the European countries amounts to 200.

597. Sweden is the country with the highest number of McDonald's restaurants per capita.

598. Antarctica is home to 90% of the fresh water in the world.

599. Utah has the highest birthrate in the United States, 21 babies per 1000 people.

600. Vermont has the slowest birthrate in the United States, 10 babies per 1000 people.

601. A baby's head is a quarter the size of the body whereas an adult's head is one eighth the size of the body.

602. The youngest person to ever give birth was a 5-year old Peruvian girl, Lina Medina, on May 14, 1939.

603. Access to Internet was declared as a human right by the United Nations in 2011; disconnecting people from it is against the international law.

604. Don Johnson won $6 million in a single night from one casino by playing Blackjack. He's been banned from Atlantic City Casinos since.

605. Cats don't meow at each other, just at humans. They hiss, purr, and spit at other cats.

606. China used more cement in the last 3 years than the US did in the entire 20th century.

607. A 19-year-old British resident legally changed his name from George Garratt to Captain Fantastic Faster Than Superman Spiderman Batman Wolverine The Hulk And The Flash Combined.

608. 7,000,000,000,000,000,000,000,000,000 is the number of atoms an adult human being is comprised of.

609. The only person to have 5 stars on the walk of fame is Gene Autry. His categories include: Film, TV, Radio, Music and Live Performances.

610. The most fertile age for women is 22.

611. Skiing was a common form of transportation and recreation in Ancient Russia and among Vikings.

612. Prince Charles and prince William never travel on the same plane as a precaution.

613. In lucid dreaming, you are aware of your dreams and have control over it.

614. Zohnerism is the use of a true fact to lead a scientifically ignorant public to a false conclusion.

615. The Titanic wreckage is being corroded by a unique type of bacteria, and it is estimated that the ship will exist for another 12 years before its completely gone.

616. A laser removal technique helps break down the tattoos so that the white blood cells help carry it away. You poop out your tattoo.

617. Babies have gills when they are in the womb to help them breath in the water that they swim in; the gills go away before the birth.

618. A lifespan of a fox is about 2-5 years.

619. Pigs can be as smart as a three-year-old human

620. 68 million trees are used every year to produce paper in US.

621. Dogs have a high emotional intelligence.

622. Saudi Arabia is the largest country that doesn't have a river.

623. Zerao is a stadium in Brazil in which the midfield line supposedly lies exactly on the Equator, making each team defend one hemisphere.

624. Walmart is the largest employer in the United States, with 2.2 million people employed.

625. Army is the second largest employer in the United States with about one million people employed by the army.

626. You cannot overdose on smoking weed.

627. There are ants that can explode to take down enemies.

628. A human baby possesses 60 additional bones than an adult.

629. Women experience less depression after a breakup than men.

630. Frisbee inventor was cremated and crafted into frisbees after his death.

631. Whatsapp and Facebook Messengers have the capability to manage 60 billion messages per day.

632. Of all the US high school football players only 1 in 4,233 eventually make it to the NFL.

633. The northern leopard frog uses its eyes to devour its prey and push it down to its throat to swallow it.

634. All four types of tea - black, green, white, and oolong - come from the same plant, *Camellia Sinensis.*

635. Originally tea was used as medicine and it took about 3000 years for it to become an everyday drink.

636. 1,700 villagers and 3,500 livestock were killed overnight because of a lake in Africa that released 300,000 tons of carbon dioxide. Everything within 16 miles was suffocated. Scientists still do not understand what the cause was.

637. An Ottoman Sultan sent his navy to rescue Jews expelled from Spain in 1492.

638. Laron syndrome is a genetic mutation that guarantees longer life expectancy, immunity to cancer and diabetes, and a shorter stature.

639. There are more Rolls Royces in Hong Kong than anywhere else in the world.

640. The most popular tea in the United States in 1800s was green tea, but after World War II, the United States started importing tea from India which produced black tea, hence the black tea became more popular.

641. The liver of a polar bear contains more vitamin A than the human body can tolerate; so, if you eat it, you will likely die.

642. Tea was used as a form of currency in ancient China.

643. A large tree can produce enough oxygen to support four people for the whole day.

644. The first air-conditioned car was built in Detroit by the Packard Motor Car Company in 1939.

645. Beetles are categorized into 380,000 different species covering up almost 40% of the insects on earth.

646. Roger Fisher, a Harvard professor, proposed implanting nuclear launch codes in a volunteer so that the President would have to kill an innocent person before firing. The Pentagon rejected the idea fearing the President would not go through with it even if it was necessary.

647. 'Abracadabra' is a term that comes from the Aramaic, an ancient Hebrew, phrase meaning "I create as I speak".

648. It takes 100,000 miles of blood vessels for the blood to completely circulate in a human body.

649. The first Oscar Award took place in 1929 with only 270 people in attendance and only 15 awards to distribute.

650. Before 1857 there was a half penny and it was worth more than a dime in today's money. It was discontinued because US thought that it was worth too little.

651. Polar bears are capable of eating 86 penguins in one go.

652. Amazon rainforest produces about 20 percent of the world's supply of oxygen.

653. Did you know that trees help cool down the air? It's the shadow of the trees that cools down the surface and the air.

654. Turning your left cheek towards the camera makes you more attractive.

655. The proper spelling for a donut is doughnut, but the newer spelling is also acceptable.

656. Some trees can grow in 10 to 15 years, whereas others take 25 to 30 years to grow.

657. Up to 30 percent of the surface of the Earth is covered with trees.

658. Ethiopian calendar has 13 months.

659. The Amazon Basin contains one fifth of the world's fresh water.

660. Your body will start burning fat instead of carbs if you exercise in the morning because your body used up carbs while you were asleep.

661. A sponge is classified as an animal and it does not have a brain nor a central nervous system.

662. Almost 10 percent of adults aged 50 and up smoke recreational marijuana in the US.

663. Harry Potter has the same birthday as J. K. Rowling, July 31.

664. A U.S. army burns through 22 gallons of fuel per soldier per day, but in World War II it was only 1 gallon per soldier per day.

665. With each passing year, Finland is said to be getting 7km.sq bigger due to rebounding of the ice glaciers into the sea.

666. A fake painting of Goya was sold for 1.5 million euro. The two brothers who sold it later found out that the money was counterfeit.

667. Around 78% of brands take only one hour to respond to a query on Twitter.

668. Hans Steininger held the record of having the longest beard in 1567. He died by tripping over his own beard while running from a fire.

669. Pepsi's Naked Juice has a higher sugar content than an equivalent amount of Pepsi Cola even though the juice is marketed as "healthy".

670. Insects have no respiratory system, they breathe through the bloodstream.

671. An adult human body possesses enough iron to create a 3 inches long nail.

672. A quarter of all lobsters are born with a genetic defect that gives them a blue color, making them more visible to predators in the oceans.

673. A Giving Pledge is a promise by rich people to give away most of their wealth when they die; some of them are Elon Musk, Warren Buffet, Mark Zuckerberg, Bill Gates, and Sir Richard Branson.

674. Blind people have more vivid dreams than regular people and their dreams are enhanced by other senses.

675. There are over 130 pyramids in Egypt.

676. Muhammad Ali requested to place his star on the wall rather than on the Walk of Fame's sidewalk because he didn't want anyone to step on his name due to religious reasons.

677. Consistently farting for 6 years and 9 months can generate enough gas to build an atomic bomb.

678. Baltic Sea and The North Sea are joined seas; however, they don't mix up with one another and have different colors due to different densities.

679. According to a 2011 study, every day more than 3.2 billion images are being shared on social media.

680. The damage from cigarette smoking shows up in minutes not years.

681. You can find rainforests even in Alaska and Canada.

682. 25 percent of all cars in the world are produced in China.

683. Mexico is officially known as the United Mexican States.

684. A puma, cougar, and mountain lion are all the same exact animal.

685. One of the results of the French Revolution was to switch all measures of time from base 12 to base 10 including a 10-day week. This experiment lasted for only 12 years.

686. The first settlement in Alaska was established by Russians in 1784.

687. United States purchased Alaska in 1867 for $7,200,000, or 2 cents per acre.

688. 25 percent of all oil produced in the United States comes from Alaska.

689. Sometimes Apple makes their employees work on fake projects until they can be trusted.

690. The highest mountain in North America is Mt. McKinley located in Alaska.

691. Alaska is derived from an Eskimo word Alakshak which means great lands or peninsula.

692. Cubans were not allowed to own cell phones until 2008.

693. Griffinfly is the largest insect to ever fly in the sky, having a wingspan of 2.5 feet.

694. There are tiny mites living in our eyelashes.

695. Hal Roach was a famous director who used to hire drunk and insane people to generate creative ideas.

696. To attract female goats, Billy goats urinate on their own heads.

697. Jewish people do not eat pork.

698. Khazaria was a medieval Turkic kingdom that adopted Judaism as its official religion; it was the only non-Semitic state to become Jewish after Israel.

699. The largest economy in the United States is California.

700. More deer are killed by drivers than by hunters.

701. The automotive center of the world is in Detroit.

702. If the earth were ever to stop spinning, all the oceans would flow to the north and south poles.

703. Around 16 to 20 percent of the terms searched on Google are said to have been never searched before.

704. Bamboo can grow 35 inches per day making it the fastest growing woody plant in the world.

705. The heaviest insect found on the earth is 'Giant Weta'. It weighs more than a pound and is found in New Zealand.

706. The CIA is expected to release the JFK assassination records to the public no later than 10/26/2017.

707. The jaw muscle is the strongest muscle found in the human body.

708. On average, humans spend about 6 years of their life sleeping.

709. The population of the United States is only five percent of the total world population, but Americans use up to 30 percent of the world's paper.

710. More plastic has been produced in the past 10 years than in the last century.

711. You can detect the smell of the skunk as far as a mile away.

712. Ethiopia has never been occupied by a foreign country even though Italy tried twice.

713. You can take out insurance against being abducted by aliens, more than 40,000 Americans have done it.

714. Brain messages can travel up to 200 miles per hour (322 km per hour) through the nerves.

715. Tigers are one of the most vengeful animals on the planet and they can and will take revenge on those who have wronged them.

716. Only about 0.1 percent of DNA reflects the differences of each human individual.

717. The human DNA is 10 billion miles long and can stretch from Earth to Pluto and back.

718. The first motorcycle was built in Germany in 1885.

719. It had cost $21,000 to put up the famous 'Hollywoodland' sign in 1923 which was reduced to Hollywood after 18 months.

720. A kangaroo cannot hop if someone carries its tail off the ground.

721. If gold was to be extracted from the oceans, each human would get approximately 9 pounds of the yellow metal.

722. 0.01% of the world's electricity is used by Google to manage all the searches.

723. The word "Muggle" from the Harry Potter series means a person without magical ability, and it was added to the Oxford English Dictionary in 2003.

724. In Ancient Athens about 40 to 80 percent of the population was slaves.

725. Drinking too much water can lead to excessive sweating, urination, and even death.

726. Three of the African states are kingdoms; they are Lesotho, Morocco, and Swaziland.

727. Lesotho is a "mountain kingdom" because two thirds of it is covered by mountains.

728. The national cloth of Lesotho is a blanket which acts against cold and is worn as a symbol of status; it comes with colorful patterns.

729. The peak of Eiffel Tower tends to deviate 7 inches away from the sun because the metal expands while being exposed to the sun.

730. Termite queens are capable of laying 6,000 to 7,000 eggs in a single day.

731. People who have excessive body hair tend to be more intelligent than people who do not have any body hair.

732. The leading cause of drowning is water.

733. There are 30 types of kisses a human can try.

734. The light that blinks at the top of the Capitol Records Tower spells Hollywood when converted into Morse code.

735. J. K. Rowling wrote the first ideas about Harry Potter on a napkin traveling on a train to London.

736. To initiate the process of sleep, your body temperature drops.

737. The temperature of water where the Titanic sank was -2 degrees Celsius.

738. You would need to walk an entire length of a football field to burn the calories received from one M&M candy.

739. Porsche is the world's most profitable automobile manufacturer.

740. The most common chromosomal abnormality is the Down Syndrome.

741. The largest pyramid in Egypt was built from two million stone bricks and each stone brick weighs two and a half tons.

742. Some historians think that America was discovered by Amerigo Vespucci before Christopher Columbus because of a letter that is dated 1497.

743. About 80 languages are spoken in Ethiopia. Oromo and Amharic are the most widely spoken languages. English and Arabic are also widely spoken.

744. US - Canada border is the longest border in the world.

745. Ants use chemical messengers to talk to each other; they can signal danger or let everyone know where the food is.

746. At the equator you would weigh less than you would at the poles.

747. An average car is assembled in 25 hours, 10 of which are used to paint the car.

748. There are more skyscrapers in Hong-Kong than anywhere else in the world.

749. The largest landlocked country in the world is Kazakhstan.

750. The president of Mongolia attended the Harvard University.

751. In Sweden, the price of a speeding ticket is based on the person's salary; the highest ticket ever issued was $1,000,000 for driving at 180 mph.

752. The Mongolian capital, Ulaanbaatar, is the coldest capital in the world with an average temperature of -1 degrees Celsius.

753. A family in Kentucky had blue skin due to a rare genetic condition called methemoglobinemia.

754. The smallest insect on the earth is found in Costa Rica and goes by the name of fairyfly. It is only 0.014 cm in length.

755. Our ears and nose never stop growing.

756. Harry Potter and the Order of the Phoenix suffered a $167 million loss on paper.

757. In America, every year around 8,000 people are injured because of musical instruments.

758. A third of cat owners think that their cats can read their minds.

759. Apples are more efficient at waking you up in morning than coffee.

760. A bee will die if it must use its stinger.

761. Bees are the only insects whose food the humans can eat.

762. About 97 percent of DNA is "non-coding" and its function is unknown.

763. The state in between being awake and asleep is known as hypnagogia.

764. About 3 percent of people in the US have a mental disability.

765. According to one of the surveys in 2009 the worst drivers were in New York and New Jersey.

766. The amount of study done on Mars is of such extent that today we have more detailed maps of Mars' lands than we have of Earth's oceans.

767. Six new profiles are being made on Facebook every second. That makes 500,000 every day.

768. Haskell Free Library and Opera House, is built on the US-Canada border, and has two addresses, one American and one Canadian.

769. Onthophagus Taurus can pull 1141 times of its own bodyweight.

770. A human eye can recognize 10 million distinct colors.

771. Most of the cancer is caused by environmental factors, and only about 5 to 10 percent are inherited genetics.

772. Google rents goats to mow the grass outside their headquarters as part of the green initiative.

773. Brains constantly predict what other people are about to say before they say it.

774. When you see a television commercial of milk, you are most likely seeing a mixture of white paint and a thinner.

775. Every week, Google acquires one company on average.

776. The donuts are a $3.6 billion industry in the United States.

777. Google is worth about $300 billion today, but it was almost sold at $1 million in 1999 to the person who rejected the offer.

778. Civilian deaths caused by police are 30,000 percent more likely to occur in the US than in the UK.

779. The most popular type of a donut is a glazed donut.

780. If you spend a large amount of time with someone, you literally start picking up their habits.

781. In 2014 a beard of Tutankhamun's golden mask fell off during the cleaning process in the Egyptian Museum. The workers tried to glue it but because the permanent damage has already been done they were prosecuted for this in 2016.

782. Americans used to spend $6 billion on fast food in 1970; this number rose to $200 billion in 2014.

783. The only country that doesn't sell Coca-Cola and PepsiCo products is North Korea.

784. The most common drug in the world is caffeine; its side effects include infertility, muscle weakness, and heart irregularities.

785. The part that stimulates fear and anxiety in women, called amygdala, tends to shut down when they are in the middle of an orgasm.

786. Kevin Fast is a Canadian who holds the record of pulling the heaviest aircraft which weighed 188.8 tons.

787. Hitler's mother wanted to have an abortion but the doctors insisted her to keep the baby.

788. The word "idiot" originates from Greek meaning someone who did not participate in politics and public affairs.

789. A 15-inch large snowflake was recorded once, making it the largest snowflake ever.

790. The suicide rate in America is around 30,000 per year.

791. One of the longest lines to McDonald's was a line of cars seven miles long in Kuwait when the first McDonald's restaurant opened.

792. The tallest documented person in the world is Robert Pershing Wadlow at 2.72 m (8 ft 11.1 in)

793. The deepest point on earth is the Mariana Trench located in the Pacific Ocean, it is about 11 kilometers in depth; you could place the tallest mountain on earth, Mount Everest, and it would still be 2 kilometers below the sea level.

794. The brain is only 3 percent of the body's weight, but it consumes 20 percent of the energy.

795. Studies say that a person can't dream while he/she is snoring.

796. During the 16th and 17th centuries, the source of Denmark's income (about 2/3rd) came from letting people enter and leave the Baltic sea. Those who couldn't pay were sunk.

797. In Ancient Egypt, one of the battles was lost because the enemy used cats against them; Egyptians refused hurting cats as they were seen sacred.

798. Over 391 million accounts on Twitter have zero followers.

799. The Romans used urine to brighten and whiten their teeth in the early days.

800. It took 2 hours and 40 minutes for the RMS Titanic to sink after hitting the iceberg.

801. In Russia there is a village called Paris where they built a 1:5 replica of the Eiffel Tower in 2005.

802. Vikings used to take a bath at least once a week, that is more frequently than their other European contemporaries.

803. The monetary currency of Afghanistan is known as Afghanis.

804. About half of all the plants and animals live in the rainforests which cover only two percent of the surface.

805. Pogonophobia is a fear of beards.

806. European diseases killed 20 million Mexicans in just five years.

807. The teeth are considered a part of the skeleton too.

808. According to various studies, the oldest insect remains found date back some 400 million years ago. This makes them even older than dinosaurs.

809. More than 50% of suicides in America are carried out by firearms.

810. There are more than 3 million shipwrecks still to be found under the oceans, as per the United Nations.

811. You can use YouTube in 76 various languages, which covers around 95% of the world's population

812. Researchers have found a way to reduce the sugar content of candy bars by 40 percent without affecting the taste; it will likely be used in consumer chocolates starting in 2018.

813. Humans are the only mammals who can willingly delay the sleep.

814. In 1962, Tanganyika (now called Tanzania) suffered from a laughter epidemic which lasted for more than a year. Many people were affected with additional symptoms of farting, crying, pain and rashes.

815. A human heart can produce enough energy to run a truck for 32 km.

816. According to surveys, 95% of people don't have the guts to say in person what they say in texts.

817. The internet cables lying under the oceans are merely 2.7 inches in width.

818. The most common cause of suicide in the US is untreated depression.

819. There are more than 400 million active users on Instagram.

820. Roy. C. Sullivan, a former US Park Ranger, was hit by lighting a total of seven times, and survived each.

821. About 87 years ago BBC had a day when they had no news to report at all, so they just played piano music.

822. In the earliest US elections, the President could not choose his vice president, it was the candidate with the second most vote.

823. About 70 percent of all emails sent is spam.

824. The fangs of an Australian Funnel-Web spider can penetrate fingernails and shoes.

825. Natural selection favors shorter girls.

826. 30 percent of Americans don't drink alcohol at all, 80 percent drink less than 1 drink a week. The top 10 percent drinks about 74 drinks a week.

827. The existence of UFO's is formally recognized by France, Italy and Chile.

828. At one point in history the East India Trading Company had a private army of 260,000 which is double of what the British army had.

829. More than 65,000 Japanese are 100 years of age or older.

830. Cats decided to live with humans on their own and domesticated themsclves.

831. The island of Kiribati is being evacuated by the government because it is slowly sinking into the oceans due to rapid climate change.

832. A home with a view to the water such as an ocean can make you calmer, happier, and more creative.

833. Out of 176 million accounts on Pinterest, only a hundred million are active.

834. The only British soldier to kill an enemy with a longbow during World War II is Lt. Col. "Mad" Jack Churchill. He insisted his general to let him go to battle carrying medieval weapons.

835. When a person focuses on other people's negative qualities, they are likely to possess those same qualities.

836. An adult's digestive system is 9 meters in length, starting from the mouth and ending at the anus.

837. Some insects can enjoy a 360-degree field view due to the presence of ommatidia.

838. The rate of committing suicides in males is much more than in females. Around 79% of men do suicides while women are more likely to have just suicidal thoughts.

839. There are altogether seventeen various words for ‘surrender’ in the French language.

840. The Spanish Inquisition gave a 30-day notice before coming to get someone.

841. There is a fish that can jump out of water and stab somebody with a speed of 37 MPH, with multiple human fatalities on record.

842. Our hearts can beat even after they’re separated from the body because they beat on electrical impulses that are generated inside the heart.

843. A crocodile is incapable of poking its tongue out of its mouth.

844. More than 3 million companies in the US have made LinkedIn accounts, out of which only 17% of accounts belong to small businesses.

845. The fastest fly till date is a male horsefly, belonging to the Hybomitra specie. It can fly up to 145 km per hour.

846. There are some glaciers in Antarctica that pour red liquid giving the impression of bleeding, for which they are named ‘Blood Falls’.

847. Your brain continues to be in a developing stage until you reach 40 years of age.

848. Facebook has around 81 million fake profiles.

849. Japanese think that once a cat dies it turns into a superpower spirit. In a Buddhist believe the cat's body is considered a temporary resting place for very spiritual people.

850. There exists a special limestone wall in Bolivia with dinosaur footprints that are some 68 million years old.

851. The longest crocodile ever recorded was found in 1957 in Australia and was about 28 feet long.

852. Not a single engineer working on the Titanic survived.

853. A man managed to accumulate $50,000 penny by penny by making fake accounts and stealing from the two step verification deposits.

854. The 23rd Bomb Squadron managed to save the city of Hilo by dropping bombs to force the volcanic lava to change its course.

855. According to a Canadian research, women's hearts tend to beat faster than men's hearts.

856. In 2007, Iran's government caught 14 squirrels near a nuclear plant thinking they were spying on them.

857. More than 300 million cells in our body get destroyed every minute. This means that you just lost 50,000 cells just while reading this sentence.

858. While working on the rabies antidote, Luis Pasteur ordered to be shot in the head if he or his assistant got infected.

859. Mahatma Gandhi was nominated 5 times for the Nobel Peace Prize but never won any.

860. Saudi Arabia imports both sand and camels from Australia.

861. The first king of Belgium was German, fought in the Russian army, married an English princess and had previously turned down the chance to become a king of Greece.

862. In 2011, a woman called Aimee Davison bought a piece of art for $10,000 that only resided in the artist's head.

863. In Jamaica, males are prohibited to have sex with one another. If caught, they are imprisoned for 10 years.

864. Hitler, Napoleon, and Alexander the Great feared cats.

865. Wearing headphones for more than an hour causes the bacteria in our ears to multiply by 700 times.

866. Your brain has an unlimited storage capacity and it cannot be used up like the computer RAM.

867. So far only a single space satellite has been destroyed by an asteroid.

868. Motion detectors do not work if the walls are too hot.

869. It takes two weeks for sloths to completely digest their food.

870. During World War II, the Oscar trophies given to actors were made of wood because metal was scarce.

871. You can prevent crying while peeling or cutting onions by chewing gum.

872. The longest word in the English Language that is in alphabetical order is “Almost”.

873. Your fingernails grow 4 times faster than the toenails.

874. The national anthem of Bosnia has no lyrics.

875. Writing with red ink in Portugal is considered as a rude attitude.

876. The only living thing that has no heart, no bones, and no brain is the jellyfish.

877. The average number of hairs you lose on a daily basis is 100 to 125.

878. With the human sense of hearing, it is possible to interpret a sound within 0.05 seconds.

879. Green eyes are said to be the rarest as only 2% of the entire population has green eyes.

880. Venus and Uranus are the only two planets to rotate backwards on their axis.

881. Fredric Baur was the inventor of Pringles can. His ashes were buried inside a pringle can when he died.

882. Starfish have the capability to regenerate their whole body.

883. Facebook developers wanted to name the "Like" button, the "Awesome" button.

884. Sea horses are always in search of mates and when they find one, they travel holding each other's tails.

885. The Honduran city of Yoro is famous for its "Rain of Fish" event where fish rain from the sky.

886. A mosquito possesses 47 teeth in its mouth.

887. Our sense of smell and taste decreases by 20% - 50% when we are travelling on a plane.

888. Goats, hippos, and horses have rectangular eyes.

889. Our sneeze completes 30 feet, and travels at a speed of 100 miles an hour.

890. A sloth is so lazy that it would take him around a month to travel a mile.

891. Newly born babies are color blind. They only see in black and white, however, the color vision begins to develop after a week.

892. When we talk to the people that we like, our voice changes.

893. Toronto was the first ever city to introduce the computerized traffic system.

894. The owner of Macy's died on the Titanic. He refused to get in a lifeboat before women and children, and his wife refused to leave without him. She said, "I will not be separated from my husband. As we have lived, so will we die, together." They were last seen standing on the deck, arm in arm.

895. There was a man with a severe OCD and a phobia of germs; he attempted to commit suicide by shooting himself in the head. The shot did not kill him, but it did eliminate his illness without leaving any other brain damage.

896. The greatest number of brains found in a living being is a leech. It has 32 brains.

897. Symbolics was the first ever domain name registered on the web.

898. Grapes explode when put in a microwave oven.

899. Nutella was invented during the World WAR II.

900. There was only one student (Sam) who graduated in New Mexico's first graduating class but was shot before the graduation ceremony.

901. Back in 1979, homosexuality was considered an illness in Sweden.

902. A busy bee produces about 1/12 of a teaspoon of honey in its entire life.

903. The only continent where reptiles and snakes aren't found is the Antarctica.

904. The fear of ducks is known as Anatidaephobia.

905. There are some restaurants in Germany that fine customers who don't finish the food.

906. Cristiano Ronaldo once donated his entire salary ($83k) for the surgery of a boy who was suffering from a form of a brain disorder.

907. Walter Arnold was the first person to be given a speeding ticket. He was going at a speed of 8 mph in an area which allowed 2 mph.

908. Colonel Sanders, the owner of KFC, worked at a gas station before the establishment of KFC.

909. The speed of a flea at the start of a jump is greater than the speed of a spaceship in the orbit.

910. Lemons and limes come from the same tree.

911. Bees kill more people than all the poisonous snakes combined.

912. The air pollution indoors is 2-5 times higher than the outdoors air.

913. The silk of black widow is said to be stronger than platinum and steel. It was used to make guns during the World War II.

914. Fuggerei is a village in Germany where the rent hasn't increased since 1520 and is still 88 euro cents for a year.

915. The fastest insects are the cockroaches and they can run at the speed of 6.5 km per hour or 4 mph.

916. The dumbest animal in the history of planet Earth was Stegosaurus. It weighed about 3 tons, but its brain was the size of a walnut.

917. A TV show in Iceland called "Keeping up with the Kattarshians" is aired 24/7 that involves cats living in a tiny model house.

918. Pablo Escobar once burned $2 million to produce fire because his daughter was feeling cold.

919. Harry Patch was the last World War I surviving soldier who died at the age of 111.

920. There's a jellyfish called Lion's Mane which is larger than a blue whale.

921. You can't block the profile of Facebook's founder (Mark Zuckerberg).

922. Jackie Chan stayed in his mother's womb for 12 months and had to be surgically removed.

923. Women lose about 1.73 billion bobby pins every year.

924. 95 percent of all known living organisms on earth are the invertebrates.

925. A goat's milk has five times less fat than a cow's milk, and it takes one hour to digest a cow's milk whereas goat's milk takes only 20 minutes.

926. "Psi-traveling" is the cat's ability to find a way back home. This could be done by using the angle of the sun, or through specific magnetized cells that act like a compass.

927. The picture on Pink Floyd's album "A Momentary Lapse of Reason" had actual 700 beds in the picture, none of them were cutouts.

928. Sharks do not get sick.

929. There was a suicide bomber who was planning to detonate in Moscow at New Year's Eve using her cell phone as a trigger. The bomb detonated when her mobile company sent her a spam email, killing only herself.

930. An American soldier Jeremy Morlock admitted that he killed unarmed Afghanistan civilian for sport as a part of 'kill team' while he was deployed overseas.

931. The only organ in a human that doesn't have blood supply is the cornea. It gets oxygen from the external air.

932. The most expensive painting ever to be sold was Pablo Picasso's nude which was sold for $106.5 million.

933. Famous Harry Potter series author J.K Rowling lost her billionaire status because she gave away hefty amounts of money to charities.

934. Big Bertha, a gun used during the World War I, was so powerful that soldiers had to be at a 300-yard distance and keep their ears, eyes and nose shut or its sound would injure them.

935. Mark Zuckerberg suffers from red-green blindness; therefore, Facebook's primary color is blue.

936. In Ireland, Iceland, Greenland, and Antarctic there are no snakes.

937. Christian Bale managed to lose 63 pounds in 4 months to fit the role in the movie The Machinist, following immediately, he gained 100 pounds in just 6 months for Batman Begins.

938. Butterflies taste the food with their paws.

939. Basenji is the only type of a dog that doesn't know how to bark.

940. Squirrels cover their bodies with their tail when it snows.

941. In China, Twitter, Facebook and The New York Times have been banned since 2009.

942. Queen Elizabeth I used to take a bath only once in every three months because back in the day, people of London thought that immersion in water was dangerous.

943. There's a waterfall in Oahu, Hawaii, called Waipuhia Falls where water flows upward instead of flowing downwards.

944. Dolphins sleep with one open eye.

945. Despite being the CEO of Facebook, Mark Zuckerberg only receives a salary of $1 per month.

946. When a male and a female mantis have sex, the female rips off the male's head.

947. Mostly, yellow color is used for highlighting text because it doesn't create a shadow when photocopied.

948. Brian Acton, the co-founder of Whatsapp, was turned down for a job by Facebook in 2009, in 2014 Facebook purchased this app 'Whatsapp' for $19 billion.

949. Smiling is said to improve your immune system.

950. The only flower which is also a vegetable is broccoli.

951. Facebook operates on 61 million lines of code which is twice the code ran in a F-35 Fighter jet.

952. The only bird that cannot fly yet swim is the penguin.

953. In 2016, a bug in the Instagram app was found by a 10-year-old boy for which he was awarded $10,000 by Facebook.

954. Pudu deer is the world's smallest deer and can weigh up to 26 lbs.

955. James Cameron sold The Terminator for $1, on condition that he be the director.

956. Raccoons can solve complex problems such as opening complex locks and remembering the solution to tasks for up to 3 years.

957. A baboon was once hired as a signalman and continued to work the position until his death, without making a single mistake.

958. A British man named Simon Smith legally changed his name to 'Bacon Double Cheeseburger' in 2015.

959. The demand for adult diapers is higher than the demand for baby diapers in Japan.

960. The vast majority of Muslims are not Arabs.

961. If a Hawaiian woman puts flowers behind her ears, she lets others know that she is available. The more flowers that she has, the stronger is her desire.

962. We forget more than 90% of our dreams in just 10 minutes after waking up.

963. Most number of suicides are witnessed on Valentine's day.

964. In 2016, 1 out of every 8 couples in the US met at an online dating website.

965. When refrigerated, rubber bands last longer.

966. There are 293 distinct ways to get change for a single dollar.

967. Goldfish has a memory span of only three seconds.

968. On average, children laugh about 400 times a day, whereas the adults laugh about 15 times a day.

969. "The Quick Brown Fox Jumps Over The Lazy Dog" is a sentence in the English language where all the 26 alphabets are used.

970. Vatican is the smallest country in the world, built on just 108.7 acres.

971. Floyd Mayweather is the highest paid athlete with a per hour rate of $87,500,000.

972. 90% of all mobile phones sold in Japan are waterproof due to the youth's habit of using the device while showering.

973. Japan used fleas infested with Bubonic China during World War II.

974. Black cats are considered a good luck charm in Japan.

975. Horses can sleep while standing up.

976. A cat cannot chew large chunks of food because its jaw does not move sideways.

977. Two thirds of people kiss with closed eyes, whereas the other one third observe the emotions of their partners.

978. Apple, the company name, came from Steve Job's likeness for apple, the fruit.

979. Mobile phones are said to contain more bacteria than a toilet seat.

980. Basketball shorts were usually short, until Michael Jordan requested them to be longer.

981. The average NBA player can jump as high as 28 inches.

982. Grapes are a kind of berries.

983. In 2004, Pepsi and Coca Cola were used by farmers in India instead of pesticides because they did the job just as well for a cheaper cost.

984. The Hogwarts Express from the Harry Potter series is a real train in Scotland.

985. One of the side effects of some antidepressants is taking away a person's ability to "feel love."

986. Caterpillars have 248 muscles in the head.

987. Your mouth gets filled with extra saliva just before you're about to vomit to protect your mouth from harmful acids in the vomit.

988. People who use "like" frequently in their conversations are more thoughtful and more aware of their surroundings.

989. Cashew nuts can eliminate bacteria that causes tooth decay, acne, and TB.

990. There are more English speakers in China than in the entire US.

991. Eating large amounts of chocolate can kill your dog because it contains theobromine that dogs can't metabolize.

992. On April Fool's Day, Google's employees received an email that warned them of a python at loose in the company's New York Office. The news turned out to be true.

993. Miley Cyrus was paid $10 for picking up bras and underwear thrown by fans in her father's concert.

994. About 40 percent of people who were rejected by those they love, fall into a clinical depression.

995. Portland was named by flipping a coin. The two choices were Portland and Boston.

996. Touching stainless steel can suck in the odor of garlic and onion from your hands.

997. A Chinese man was once fined $1600 which he paid in coins. It took 18 officers and an entire day to count the money.

998. In 1972, during the Apollo 16 mission, an astronaut named Charles Duke left a family photo wrapped in plastic on the moon. The photo is still there.

999. R. Budd Dwyer shot himself live during a press conference when he was charged for conspiracy that held a 55-year prison sentence.

1000. The tentacles of a giant Antarctic jellyfish can reach 36 meters, or 120 feet.

1001. There's a panda named Qizai that has brown fur instead of black and white.

1002. A man was irritated by Eiffel Tower's light that shone in his bedroom and tried to blow up the tower.

1003. Jonathan Lee Richards holds the record of filing most lawsuits (over 4000). He even sued Guinness Book of World Records for naming him so.

1004. You are restricted to name a folder 'Con' in Microsoft Windows because it is a reserved operating system word.

1005. Pope Francis was a nightclub bouncer and had a girlfriend in the early days.

1006. Japan has the longest lifespan averaging 83.84 years.

1007. A woman in Indiana was once shot by her dog whose name was Trigger.

1008. Two out of five men marry their first love.

1009. Michael Jackson's hair were accidentally lit on fire in a Pepsi commercial. However, he didn't sue the company but asked them to fund a burn center.

1010. The speed of reproduction of rats is so big that two rats could produce a progeny of one million rats in one and a half years.

1011. Snakes never blink because their eyes are covered by thin transparent eyelids.

1012. Turkey was the first ever country to allow women to vote in the elections.

1013. The cost to feature on the Hollywood Walk of Fame is $30,000. Celebrities like Julia Roberts, Denzel Washington, Al Pacino don't have a star because they haven't paid.

1014. The last episode of Tom and Jerry shows the two characters committing suicide on a railway track.

1015. It is illegal to eat someone else's hamburger in Oklahoma.

1016. When Queen Elizabeth visited the set of Game of Thrones, she refused to sit on the throne, abiding the law of not sitting on any foreign throne.

1017. Our brain can stay alive for 4-6 minutes in the absence of oxygen.

1018. There is a store in Alabama where you can buy items found in unclaimed airport baggage.

1019. Napoleon and Hitler hold a difference of 129 years in being born, coming to power and invading Russia.

1020. Benjamin Franklin never patented any of his designs and inventions because he believed "that as we enjoy great advantages from the inventions of others, we should be glad of an opportunity to serve others by any invention of ours, and this we should do freely and generously".

1021. A Soviet Era monument in Russia, Voronezh, was destroyed when someone painted it to look like Patrick from SpongeBob.

1022. Genghis Khan ordered to be buried in an unmarked grave to keep it a secret. No one knows where he's buried even today.

1023. To fight grave robberies, coffin torpedoes were invented in 1800s. They fired if the coffin was opened.

1024. To treat their cows ethically Ben and Jerry's have them massaged.

1025. The exhaust fumes coming out of a car are the same as the chemicals making up the ink. Air Ink is a company that takes carbon emissions collected from tailpipes to make their own earth-friendly inks and markers, helping reduce the pollution caused by cars and ink making.

1026. Black-footed cat is the smallest wildcat and can weigh about 2.5 lbs. and be less than 20 inches long.

1027. The first person to explain why the sky was blue was Leonardo da Vinci.

1028. When bitten by young ones, lions pretend to be hurt just so to encourage them.

1029. Heels were invented for butchers so that they wouldn't step in blood.

1030. Most "Made in China" stickers are made in Korea.

1031. Elephants are the most emotional animals and can be seen helping other animals.

1032. Every year, the internet traffic grows by 314,000 percent.

1033. Greek Poet Hipponax used to write poetries that were so insulting that his victims (target audience) sometimes committed suicide.

1034. The Koi fish is said to have the longest lifespan averaging 200 years.

1035. Around 65% to 85% of white cats that have blue eyes are deaf. If the cat has only one blue eye, then it is more likely to be deaf on one side.

1036. Students caught cheating on exams can get a jail time of 7 years in China.

1037. Wedding rings are worn on the left ring finger because that is the only finger whose veins connect to the heart.

1038. People with Borderline personality disorder are terrified of being abandoned or left alone. Even something small like a loved one getting home late from work or going away for the weekend can trigger intense fear.

1039. Every night a person can see between four and seven dreams.

1040. The cherry blossoms in Washington are foreign plants as they were a gift from Japan to promote relations of both countries.

1041. The diameter of Betelgeuse star is greater than the orbit of planet earth around the sun.

1042. It cost seven million dollars to build the Titanic, and two hundred million dollars to make the film.

1043. Ketchup comes out from the bottle with a speed of 30 kilometers per year.

1044. Every eighth American worked at McDonald's at some point.

1045. We spend about 20-25 percent of our time in REM sleep in which we see dreams and our body is completely paralyzed to prevent us from acting out dreams.

1046. The famous Breaking Bad star Bryan Cranston was taught how to make meth by the DEA.

1047. While searching a stolen car, the Finnish police found a dead mosquito whose blood was tested to identify the thief.

1048. The sex organs of a snail are in its head.

1049. 70 percent of all boats sold are used for fishing.

1050. Adolf Dassler, who was a member of the Nazi party, founded Adidas. Adi came from his nickname while Das were the first three letters of his second name.

1051. There's a road in Corona, California that goes by the name of "Never Ending Road" because the locals believe that anyone that drives on it is never seen or heard of again.

1052. A 1947 explosion in Texas was so strong that it knocked airplanes down, killed the entire fire dept. and dropped people eleven miles away.

1053. A World War I pigeon, named Cher Ami, saved the lives of 194 men by flying continuously and delivering a message despite being shot in the breast, blinded in one eye and his leg hung from a tendon.

1054. Two thirds of a cat's day are spent sleeping which means that the cat only spends 3 years of his life awake.

1055. Crocodiles like to swallow stones. Because of this they have a better digestion and can dive deeper.

1056. The most dangerous poison comes from a king cobra.

1057. A cat is the only domesticated animal not mentioned in the Bible.

1058. Baby otters love to sleep on their mother's stomach because they feel safe that way.

1059. In 1994, it rained blobs in the town of Oakville, Washington, that made the townspeople fall sick for 3 months.

1060. An average elephant weighs less than the tongue of an average blue whale.

1061. Oprah Winfrey earns $10 a second. That makes $600 a minute, $36,000 an hour and $311,040,000 a year.

1062. When Thai officers misbehave, they are forced to wear pink hello kitty armbands as a punishment.

1063. The great albatross can sleep while flying at the speed of 40 km per hour.

1064. The singing of the blue whale can destroy your hearing.

1065. Besides being a director, producer and an actor, Jackie Chan is also a singer and has produced around 20 music albums so far.

1066. If a man jumped as high as a louse (lice), he would jump over a football field.

1067. In Ancient Egypt, the average life expectancy was 19 years, but for those who survived childhood, the average life expectancy was 30 years for women and 34 years for men.

1068. The volume of the moon is equivalent to the volume of the water in the Pacific Ocean.

1069. After the 9/11 incident, the Queen of England authorized the guards to break their vow and sing America's national anthem for Americans living in London.

1070. In 1985, lifeguards of New Orleans threw a pool party to celebrate zero drownings, however, a man drowned in that party.

1071. Men and women have different dreams. 70 percent of characters in men's dreams are other men, whereas in women its 50 percent men and 50 percent women. Men also act more aggressively in dreams than women.

1072. A polar bear has a black skin.

1073. 2.84 percent of deaths are caused by intentional injuries (suicides, violence, war) while 3.15 percent are caused by diarrhea.

1074. On average people are more afraid of spiders than they are afraid of death.

1075. A bumblebee has hairs on its eyes, helping it collect the pollen.

1076. Mickey Mouse's creator, Walt Disney feared mice.

1077. Citarum river in Indonesia is the dirtiest and most polluted river in the world.

1078. When George R R Martin saw Breaking Bad's episode called "Ozymandias", he called Walter White and said that he'd write up a character more monstrous than him.

1079. Maria Sharapova's grunt is the loudest in the Tennis game and is often criticized for being a distraction.

1080. In Mandarin Chinese, the word for "kangaroo" translates literally to "bag rat".

1081. The first product to have a barcode was a chewing gum Wrigley.

1082. Chambarakat dam in Iraq is considered the most dangerous dam in the world as it is built upon uneven base of gypsum that can cause more than 500,000 casualties, if broken.

1083. Matt Urban was an American Lieutenant Colonel who was nicknamed "The Ghost" by Germans because he always used to come back from wounds that would kill normal people.

1084. A town of Calama in Chilli has never seen a drop of rain.

1085. Halle Berry was awarded with the Razzie award for the worst actress for her role in Catwoman.

1086. In 2006, some thieves tried to steal a Koala but changed their minds because the Koala scratched the shit out of them so that they decided to grab a crocodile instead.

1087. Ten percent of Russian treasury is filled from the revenue of the sales of vodka.

1088. When Mel Blanc, the famous Looney Tunes voice actor fell into a coma, he wouldn't respond to anything, except for when the surgeon addressed him as Bugs Bunny; he replied, "Myeeh! What's up Doc?"

1089. The first bomb dropped on Berlin in World War II killed an elephant in the zoo.

1090. Japan is the world's largest seafood importer, despite it consisting of 6,800 islands.

1091. There are 10 times more termites in the world than there are humans.

1092. By weight, a hamburger is more expensive than a new car.

1093. In New Hampshire, the license plates say, "Live Free or Die" and they are made by local prisoners.

1094. The smallest bird in the world is a Colibri-bee and it is less than five centimeters in length.

1095. A two-year-old gazelle can reach a speed of 95 km per hour.

1096. The shortest war in history occurred between England and Zanzibar in 1896; Zanzibar surrendered after just 38 minutes.

1097. Scissors were invented by Leonardo da Vinci.

1098. You cannot sneeze with open eyes.

1099. Marilyn Monroe had six toes on one of her feet.

1100. Peanut butter is one of the ingredients of dynamite.

1101. A sea star has no brain.

1102. Women blink twice as much as men.

1103. The horn of a Rhinoceros is made of tightly placed hairs.

1104. The youngest Pope of Rome was 11 years old.

1105. A snail can sleep for 3 years.

1106. Octopus's blood is blue.

1107. A tiger's tongue is so rough that it can peel off paint from a wall.

1108. If a man takes a pregnancy test and it comes positive, then he is more likely to have a testicular cancer.

1109. Singer Kesha scored a perfect 1500 score in her SAT's and is said to have an IQ of 140.

1110. Hong Kong allows women to kill their husbands with their bare hands if they are caught cheating.

1111. Kidneys filter out 99% of salts in the body and reuse 95% of water.

1112. David Letterman created scholarships for students who got 'C' grade because he believed that talents aren't linked with scoring high marks.

1113. Sylvester Stallone's first acting role was in a porn movie called 'Party at Kitty and Studs.'

1114. Pandas adore bamboo sticks and they can eat around 24 to 86 pounds of bamboo sticks in a day.

1115. The eruption of Krakatoa was the loudest sound ever heard and it went around the Earth three times.

1116. The oldest monarchy in the world is Japan's Yamato dynasty.

1117. When a railway line was being built in Uganda, two Tsavo lions killed 135 workers at night.

1118. Watermelon, a fruit, is a state vegetable of Oklahoma.

1119. The oldest breed of cat is the Egyptian Mau. In ancient Egyptian, mau means cat.

1120. There's a bell at Oxford University which has been functional for 175 years. No one knows the type of battery used in the device.

1121. Over 80 wands were broken by Daniel Radcliffe while filming Harry Potter because he used them as drumsticks during breaks.

1122. During old times, Egyptians used to sleep on neck supports rather than pillows to preserve their hairstyles.

1123. It takes around 200 muscles to blink with one eye.

1124. The record for doing most push-ups was set by a Japanese man called Minoru Yoshida in 1980. He did 10,507 nonstop push-ups.

1125. While filming for Lara Croft: Tomb Raider, Angelina Jolie had no stunt double. She did her stunts on her own.

1126. Sheep are said to self-medicate when they are ill and eat only a few selective plants which are good for their health.

1127. Mike Tyson decided to become a boxer after a bully killed one of his pigeons in front of him.

1128. A caterpillar has more muscles than a human being does.

1129. The weakest sense among the 5 senses of a human is the sense of taste.

1130. There are 43 giant president sculptures present in Virginia's President Park.

1131. Ryan Gosling was approached by Backstreet Boys to be a part of the band but instead, he chose acting as a career.

1132. Most of the Koreans don't have armpit odor because they lack a special type of gene that causes it.

1133. The main purpose of eyebrows is to block sweat and other debris from falling into the eyes.

1134. Every second, 1000 comments are being posted on Instagram.

1135. Shakira's school teacher stopped her from participating in the school's choir in 2nd grade thinking that she sounded like a goat.

1136. Despite being colorblind, Emerson Moser crafted 1.4 billion crayons for Crayola.

1137. The world-famous game Candy Crush makes around $850,000 in a day.

1138. Around 813 men, 27 helicopters and a nuclear bomb were sent by the United States of America to cut down a tree in Korean DMZ.

1139. In a Brazil prison, sentences of convicts can be reduced if they decide to pedal on cycles that generate energy to light up the town.

1140. There are higher chances of you dying due to a lack of sleep than due to a lack of food.

1141. According to Robert Downey Jr., it was Burger King that made him quit drugs.

1142. Squirrels and honeybees have the same amount of hair on them, that is approximately 3 million, while humans have approximately 100,000 hairs on their bodies.

1143. The 7 deadly sins inspired the SpongeBob director to create the characters. Mr. Krabs displays greed. SpongeBob displays lust. Squidward displays wrath. Sandy displays pride. Gary displays gluttony. Plankton displays envy and Patrick displays sloth.

1144. Andrej Ciesielski is a famous photographer who was arrested for taking photos of the Great Pyramid of Giza and for scaling it.

1145. The fastest growing tissue in a human body is the hair.

1146. Opossums can pass out if they get overexcited.

1147. In 1752, Ewen Macdonald was hanged but surprisingly, he sat up well and alive when brought to a surgeon for dissection.

1148. Demi Moore had to wear an eye patch to correct her vision as she was cross-eyed in her childhood.

1149. Applying sugar on a deep wound speeds up the process of healing because it increases the flow of blood.

1150. The shells of cashews contain a toxin which is like poison Ivy that is why they are sold without shells.

1151. There are 2000 taste buds in our tongue, however, we lose half of them when we reach the age of 60.

1152. It was a computer repair man who taught Taylor Swift to play the 3 chords in the guitar when she was just 12. After that she wrote her famous song, Lucky You.

1153. An experiment was conducted by King James IV in the 15th century which involved sending two infants and a mute woman to an island to learn what natural human language would be like.

1154. Tilly Smith, a 10-year-old girl, once managed to save 100 tourists and her own family by learning about tsunami in her geography lessons.

1155. Rowan Atkinson aka Mr. Bean possesses a master's degree in electrical engineering.

1156. There's a Velcro path inside an astronaut's helmet so that they could scratch their nose with it.

1157. Leonardo DiCaprio's mother named him Leonardo because when he first kicked, she was looking at a Leonardo Da Vinci's painting.

1158. There's a lake in Tanzania, Africa, called Natron, which petrifies animals when they dive in.

1159. Jennifer Lopez is the only actress to have a #1 hit album and a blockbuster movie in the same week.

1160. Gympie Gympie is a plant that produces an acid so lethal that its victims have committed suicide due to extreme pain which is like being electrocuted.

1161. In 1975, some officers in Haicheng, China, saw dogs and other animals behave differently. Around 90,000 people were evacuated from the city, and just after some time, an earthquake of 7.3 magnitude damaged 90% of the city.

1162. Seahorses are one of the deadliest predators as they have a 90% success rate when it comes to killing their prey.

1163. 4 is the only number that contains the same number of alphabets as its value.

1164. Our nose functions like an air conditioner. It warms cold air, cools hot air and blocks impurities from entering.

1165. When Frank Abagnale was caught in the movie Catch Me If You Can, the policeman who apprehended him was played by the real Frank Abagnale.

1166. Hyperion holds the record of being the tallest living tree in the world. It is 380.3 feet in length.

1167. According to the US poll, Justin Bieber is the 5th most hated man in the US.

1168. Ian McKellen and Patrick Stewart aka Magneto and Professor Xavier had no clue about how to play chess when they were shooting the chess scene at the end of the X-men 2 movie.

1169. A Thai woman once tripped in a farmyard and grabbed onto a naked electric wire and died being electrocuted. On the day of her funeral, her sister while showing to a relative how she died, also fell, grabbed the same wire, and died the same way.

1170. Elephants and humpback whales are said to undergo menopause just like female human beings.

1171. The day Michael Jackson died, popular social media platforms such as Twitter, Wikipedia and AOL Instant Messenger all crashed at 3:15pm.

1172. Cygnus is a cat that holds the record of having the longest tail among all the cats; its tail is about 44.6 cm in length.

1173. The consequence of killing someone's father in ancient Rome was a horrible death where the culprit was trapped in a large sack that had wild vipers, dogs, cocks and monkeys in it.

1174. When Norwegians get fired from their jobs or are unable to find one, the government pays them until they find a new job. It's called NAV.

1175. Arizona iced-tea costs only 99 cents because the company spends no money on advertising and believes in adapting different ways of cutting the cost.

1176. Penguins are known to push a fellow penguin into the water just to be sure if the specific area is safe to go in and free from predators.

1177. Justin Timberlake's mother served as a legal guardian for Ryan Gosling for six months.

1178. Some sea divers found a 2000-year-old Roman shipwreck in the Mediterranean Sea that was still in good condition and surprisingly, the food was also preserved in the jars.

1179. Koalas can sleep in any position they can and for 20 hours straight.

1180. There's a restaurant in Montreal which gives food free of cost to people who cannot afford to pay for the food.

1181. Cats can jump five times as high as their own height.

1182. Barn owls are said to be die-hard lovers. If their partner dies or leaves them, they lose the will to live and die too due to a heartbreak.

1183. When Jim Henson left the world, a drawing was sent to his company by Disney that showed Mickey consoling Kermit.

1184. Matthew Hogg is a British man who is drunk all the time because there is an excess of yeast in his intestine that converts all the sugary products and carbohydrates into ethanol. So, basically, his intestine makes its own alcohol.

1185. Trajan's Market was a 4-storey shopping mall in ancient Rome that had 150 shops.

1186. There are giant slides in Munich University so that students don't have to climb down to reach the ground.

1187. For human beings, giving birth is the second most painful experience while being burnt alive is the most painful of all.

1188. Besides being a terrific actor, Johnny Depp is an amazing guitarist too. He has played guitar for Marilyn Manson, Aerosmith and Oasis.

1189. The only country in the world where the entire population has access to the internet is Iceland.

1190. McLaren P1 LM is the most expensive car in the world with a price tag of $3.7 million.

1191. There is a tongue eating parasite called Cymothoa Exigua which enters a fish through gills and replaces its tongue with itself.

1192. Madonna used to work at Dunkin Donuts but was fired because she squirted jelly at a customer.

1193. A griffon vulture's egg was found at the Amsterdam Zoo but none of the vultures would accept it until the employees placed the egg in the nest of two gay vultures who immediately accepted it. Now they live as a happy family of three.

1194. Whenever Steve Jobs got stressed, he would go to the restroom and soak his feet in the company's toilet to relax.

1195. In the ancient Roman times, gladiator blood and sweat were sacred and powerful. Women used to spread gladiator sweat to enhance their beauty while emperors used to drink their blood thinking it had healing powers.

1196. There's a Sardinian cheese called casu marzu that contains live maggots in it. People close their eyes while eating it because sometimes the maggots attack the eater's eyes.

1197. It was Justin Timberlake who wrote the N-Sync-Song-Gone for Michael Jackson.

1198. A 19th century Earl called Sigurd the Mighty was killed by a man who was already dead. Sigurd beheaded a man and rode with his head on a horse but accidentally the decapitated teeth bit on Sigurd's leg and killed him due to an infection.

1199. Heights tend to increase to as much as 3% when in space because of the gaps in the discs of the vertebrate.

1200. For every human on Earth, there are a trillion stars in the known universe.

1201. The Wreck of a Titan by Morgan Robertson was published 14 years before the tragic Titanic accident, and told the story of a ship sinking due to an iceberg.

1202. Jeremy Renner was a makeup artist before he chose acting as a career.

1203. Norway's flag contains six other countries' flags in it. These include the Netherlands, Indonesia, Finland, France, Thailand, and Poland.

1204. Roman Emperor Gaius Caligula was one of the cruellest emperors. He fed prisoners to monsters and even committed incest with his sisters. He was stabbed 30 times by conspirators.

1205. When filming "I am legend", Will Smith became attached with the dog and even showed interest in buying him, but the owner refused.

1206. Earthworms are said to have five distinctive hearts in their bodies.

1207. When you scratch the inside of your ear with your finger, it produces a Pacman game like sound.

1208. The longest conflict in the history was between the Romans and the Persians which lasted for more than 721 years.

1209. Scarlett Johansson has a twin brother that goes by the name of Hunter who is also an actor by profession.

1210. Helium is the only substance that can't form into a solid shape in outer space because it is not cold enough to freeze.

1211. In Tokyo, Japan, vending machines are available at distance of every 12 meters.

1212. According to 2017 records, the title of the tallest cat in the world goes to Arcturus Aldebaran Powers which is 4 feet tall and 6.3 inches in length.

1213. When World War I commenced, the kings of Britain, Germany and Russia were all first cousins.

1214. A man built a theme park in San Antonio Texas called "Morgan's Freeland" for her disabled daughter where people with special needs are welcomed without any charges.

1215. Samuel L. Jackson is said to collect action figures of all the roles he has done in movies.

1216. Caucasian mountain shepherds are used in a Russian prison as guard dogs because they can weigh 200 pounds and have the stopping power of a .45 caliber gun.

1217. A World War I era actress named Marilyn Hare kissed 10,000 soldiers to boost their morale. She managed to pluck 733 kisses in the first day.

1218. There's a dog in Seattle called Eclipse who has a bus pass attached to her collar and catches a bus to her favorite park every day.

1219. Brad Pitt used to drive a limo for a male stripper company before he was famous.

1220. Pirates torture their enemies using the Keelhauling technique which involves tying the enemy from a rope and dragging them under the ship.

1221. Before a few hours of making Cuban cigars illegal, John. F. Kennedy bought 1200 of them.

1222. Robert Emmet Odlum was a swimming instructor and the first ever man to jump off the Brooklyn Bridge to teach people how to evacuate a building on fire, however, he died while demonstrating so.

1223. Matthew Perry, the famous F.R.I.E.N.D.S TV show starrer doesn't have a complete middle finger in his right hand. He lost a part of it in a door shutting incident in his childhood.

1224. Lenovo's CEO, Yang, received a bonus of $3 million in 2012 for the profit the company made. He distributed the bonus money among his employees and repeated the same thing in 2013.

1225. There's a law in California that lets you rescue a dog from a car if he is in danger. You won't be apprehended or punished if you break the windows. It is called the 'Right to Rescue Act'.

1226. While making the film Rocky, Sylvester Stallone asked Earnie Shavers to punch him for real. The punch caused Sylvester to vomit.

1227. You can donate your stool for science purposes and earn $13,000 per year.

1228. A woman in Arkansas once gave burials to 40 gay men in the cemetery when no one was willing to do so, not even their families.

1229. The actor who played the role of a farmer in the movie "Babe" decided to go vegan after falling in love with animals during the shoot.

1230. Aki Ra managed to diffuse 50,000 landmines using only pocket knife, hoe, stick and his hands of course after being forced by Khmer Rouge.

1231. Ken Allen, an infamous orangutan in 1980's, was known for escaping the zoo cell. He managed to escape 3 times but never escaped the premises. Other animals would take on his lead to escape, too.

1232. Prison Break star Wentworth Miller is both black and white (biracial) as his father is black and mother is white.

1233. Dick Hoyt has managed to run 255 triathlons pushing, pulling and lifting his disabled son for 37 years.

1234. When hurricane Katrina hit the US, Cuba and Venezuela were the first countries to offer their assistance by offering $1 million worth rations, but the US government rejected their help.

1235. China owns all the pandas in the world. The pandas you see in other countries are leased.

1236. In 1990 the windshield of a British airways flight was destroyed and sucked out a co-pilot, however, the main pilot held him for hours and even landed the plane safely. The co-pilot survived after sustaining multiple fractures and frostbite.

1237. There are 60% forests in Bhutan because the country's constitution says so.

1238. A couple driving to a Dave Matthews concert stopped when they saw a bicyclist with a flat tire. They reached out to help him and found out it was Dave Matthews himself. The couple got free passes, front row seats and even a dinner date with Dave Matthews.

1239. Terminator 2 had a different ending at first where Linda Hamilton grew old to watch John become the US senator. The audience and crew hated the ending so Cameron, the director, had to change it.

1240. Justin Trudeau worked as a nightclub bouncer before he became the Canadian Prime minister.

1241. Captain Robert Campbell, a British prisoner, was released on a condition that he'd return after seeing his dying mother. He kept his promise and returned after his mother died.

1242. Steve Jobs would buy a new Mercedes Benz after every 6 months because, in California, cars do not need to have number plates until they turn 6 months old.

1243. Italian High Court ruled out stealing smaller amounts of food as a crime.

1244. A Dubai resident, Mohamed Basheer, once bought a lottery ticket before getting into an Emirates plane. Unfortunately, the plane crashed but Basheer survived and even won the lottery.

1245. Steve Harvey was said to be homeless for 3 years in the early days of his career.

1246. There's a small town in southeastern Turkey that goes by the name of Batman. Its mayor Huseyin Kalkan even sued Christopher Nolan and Warner Bros for using the name Batman in their movie.

1247. Michael Jackson was supposed to attend a meeting at the World Trade Centre on 9/11 but he missed it as he was sleeping.

1248. Thousands of plants are planted by squirrels every year. Not because they want to, but because they forget where they put their acorns.

1249. London Black Cab drivers protested Uber in 2014 and caused a traffic jam around East London, however, this backfired and an 850% increase was observed in Uber App downloads.

1250. Prince Harry underwent an HIV test on live broadcast on 4th of July to demonstrate how easy it was to take an HIV test. It served as a groundbreaking moment and a 5x increase was observed in HIV self-tests.

1251. Floyd, who also went by the nickname of 'Pretty Boy', was a thief who used to destroy mortgage papers in banks so that he could free people from property debt.

1252. Stranger Things, one of Netflix's biggest hits, was turned down 15 to 20 times by various TV channels before Netflix finally aired the show on their network.

1253. Despite having one of the highest gun ownership rates in Iceland, the country has lowest crime rates in the world.

1254. NASA does not accept astronauts that are taller than 6'3".

1255. In the arctic the sun sometimes looks square when it is on the horizon.

1256. There're no such things as a bull getting angry on the sight of red color, bulls are colorblind and can only see shades of blue.

1257. Koalas turn to trees and hug them when it's very hot because trees reduce their body temperature by up to 70%.

1258. Anthony Hopkins was first approached to play for the role of Alfred, the butler, in Batman movie.

1259. Ray's Sausages owner had to spend around $30,000 because he thought there was a rotting smell coming from his sausage shop. However, it was later found that the smell was coming from the store next door where a serial killer was storing bodies of the victims.

1260. 19 prisons in Netherlands were shut down in 2013 because there was no sign of criminal activity.

1261. In 2006, 75% of Chinese people were unaware of the fact that sharks are killed to get shark fin to make shark fin soup. Today, 91% of Chinese population support the ban on killing sharks.

1262. When Nintendo's revenue declined after the failure of Wii 2 console, the CEO didn't blame the employees but encouraged them even more by cutting his own salary into half for 5 months.

1263. Women blink twice as much as men.

1264. Right handed people live nine years longer on average than the left handed.

1265. In a lifetime, an average person eats about eight spiders while sleeping.

1266. Winston Churchill was born in a woman's bathroom during a ball.

1267. The strongest muscle in the body is the tongue.

1268. In the past 4000 years no animals have been domesticated.

1269. Babies are born without a knee cap; it shows up at the age of 2-6.

1270. Every year, the Nike company pays Michael Jordan more than all the factory workers in Malaysia put together.

1271. Only one man in two billion lives to the age of 116.

1272. If you screamed for a duration of 8 years, 7 months, and 5 days, you would produce enough sound energy to heat up a cup of coffee.

1273. If Barbie was of the size of a real person, her neck would be twice as long as a normal neck.

1274. The smallest pedigree cats are the Singapura and can weigh about 4 lbs., whereas the largest cats are Main Coon cats and can weigh 25 lbs.

1275. February 1865 was the only month in the history of humanity that had no full moon.

1276. Polar bears are left handed.

1277. A catfish has more than 27,000 taste receptors, which makes it a champion in this field.

1278. Tigers have a striped skin, not just fur.

1279. A cat has 32 muscles in each of its ears.

1280. The business cards of Al Capone said that he was a seller of the furniture.

1281. A microwave oven was invented after the researcher passed through the beam and the chocolate in his pocket melted.

1282. On average, a person falls asleep in 7 minutes.

1283. A shark is the only fish that can blink with both eyes.

1284. There are more chicks on the planet than humans.

1285. Two thirds of eggplants in the world are grown in New Jersey.

1286. Dragonflies are predators and they exterminate flies, spiders, mosquitoes, and midges. During a hunt they never miss the target and overtake the prey with the probability of 98 percent.

1287. Women park the car better than the men.

1288. 90 percent of women and 75 percent of men wash their hands after using the bathroom.

1289. Every five years a woman uses enough lipstick to equal her own height.

1290. Englishmen drink more tea than anybody in the world. For example, they drink 20 times as much tea as Americans.

1291. The Ural Mountains dividing Russia into the European and Asian parts are the oldest in the world.

1292. The 1980 horror movie “Cannibal Holocaust” was so realistic, the director Ruggero Deodato was brought to court to prove that he didn’t kill his actors.

1293. The more intelligent a person is the more zinc and copper there is in his hair.

1294. Kids between the ages of 1- and 3-months cry without the tears.

1295. About 365 million people in the world have a computer, whereas a half of the world never saw or used a telephone.

1296. About 20 million people in the world have the same birthday as you.

1297. On average, the women have a higher IQ than men.

1298. Women eat a large portion of a lipstick that they use.

1299. A baby aged six-seven months can swallow and breath at the same time; adults cannot do that.

1300. If you weighed a strand of spider web long enough to encircle the earth, it would be over a pound.

1301. The higher the income of a man, the more chances that he cheats on his wife.

1302. A housemaid walks about 11 kilometers per day doing chores.

1303. Every three minutes somebody in the world reports seeing a UFO.

1304. About a fourth of the population of the world lives in China.

1305. People with blue eyes have a better vision in the dark.

1306. People that lie to you, look up-left.

1307. In western China people put salt into tea.

1308. Russia is the only country in the world that has 12 seas.

1309. About 98 percent of the Japanese are cremated after death.

1310. Every 500th person on Earth has one blue eye, and the other is brown.

1311. In a lifetime an average person spends 5 years eating.

1312. Women have a subtler sense of hearing.

1313. Giant tusker elephants have very impressive tusks that nearly scrape the ground, there are only 25 of them in the world.

1314. The most common name in the world is Muhammad.

1315. A person spends about 3 hours of his life under the water.

1316. In Kenya more than half of all people are younger than 15.

1317. Majority of boys are born in the daytime, and majority of girls are born in the night time.

1318. If a white cat is born with blue eyes, there is a 65 to 85 percent chance that it's deaf; and if only one eye is blue than that side of the ears is impaired.

1319. Tabby cats were the favorite cats of Muhammad. The M on the head of a tabby cat is said to stand for Muhammad.

1320. Men laugh longer, louder, and more frequently than women.

1321. Men release 40 percent more sweat than women.

1322. At any moment about 0.7 percent of people in the world are drunk.

1323. On average a person makes 18,000 steps per day.

1324. 80 percent of people to reach 100 years old are women.

1325. A person blinks 10 million times a year.

1326. 40 percent of Americans never visited a dentist.

1327. A new baby is born every 3 seconds.

1328. In a lifetime we eat about 27 tons of food which is equivalent to 7 elephants.

1329. In the spring children grow faster than at any other time of the year.

1330. Children fed from the breast grow to be skinnier compared to those who were raised on artificial food.

1331. Every third person in the world cannot crack his knuckles.

1332. Moscow has more billionaires than any other place in the world, that's why it is considered the most expensive city to live in.

1333. Americans spend more money on cat food than on food for children.

1334. An adult man who is doing a hard-physical work can release four liters of sweat in a day.

1335. If everyone in the world consumed as much as an average American, we would need the resources of 5 Earths to survive.

1336. Chances of giving birth to twins increase after the age of 35.

1337. Every month about 2,500 moms leave behind their newly born babies.

1338. The most dangerous job in the United States is crab fishing in Alaska.

1339. The Moscow subway is the fastest in the world, the trains are planned every 90 seconds during the surge hours.

1340. The deepest lake in the world is Baikal located in Siberia.

1341. Russia and the US are separated by just 4 kilometers (2.5 miles).

1342. In northern Thailand there are bathrooms in schools for transgender students.

1343. Mona Lisa has no eyebrows. In the Age of Renaissance in Florence it was popular for women to shave their eyebrows.

1344. A hairdryer can be used to heat up the crayon marks on the wall to be wiped out and removed.

1345. To sell a home faster and for a better price, it is enough to paint the house into a yellow color.

1346. The first yo-yo toy appeared in the 16th century in Philippines and it was used as a weapon.

1347. South Africa has the highest rates of attacks, rape, and murder with the use of firearms in the world.

1348. The percentage of people to population sitting in prison in the US is higher than anywhere else in the world.

1349. In Bolivia 5,400 serve in the navy even though the country is landlocked.

1350. If you go to the woods your pulse will slow down by about 20 beats per minute and your rate of breathing will become slower. The nervous system is stimulated, problems go away, and you calm down.

1351. If within three months the lost luggage remains unclaimed, Lufthansa company, will sell it on an auction without revealing what's inside.

1352. Billionaire Antonio Fernandez who died in August 2016, bequeathed $210 million to the residents of a village where he grew up.

1353. Throwing a shoe at a cat is equivalent to throwing a chair at a person.

1354. Thanks to the Celtic religious beliefs you could borrow money with a promise to pay back in the world of the dead.

1355. Ravens are so smart that they can tease each other.

1356. The most common lie is saying that you are doing fine.

1357. Crystals grow by reproducing themselves. In the whole world of minerals, they are the closest to being called "living".

1358. The gender of a turtle is determined by the temperature in which the egg was kept. Boys are born in the cold, and girls are born in the warm.

1359. Theoretically humans can live to an old age eating only potatoes and butter.

1360. If you stand motionless at the equator, you will be moving at a speed of 1,600 km per hour.

1361. Due to changing time zones, if you take a plane from London to New York, you will arrive two hours before you departed.

1362. Titanic was the first ship to use SOS.

1363. A Chinese millionaire destroyed all the shacks in his village and built each resident a villa.

1364. The bodies and the internal organs of the turtles do not age, that's why a turtle does not die from an old age.

1365. A human saliva contains a painkilling chemical called opiorphin which is six times stronger than morphine.

1366. Archery Tag is a sport that is like dodgeball except with foam-tipped arrows.

1367. Forgetfulness is good for the brain: the deletion of unnecessary information helps the nervous system stay flexible.

1368. When the economy is bad in the US, more laws are passed by the Congress.

1369. Raccoons wash their food before eating it.

1370. In Great Britain you can get a job waiting in line; it pays 20 British Pounds per hour (or 26 USD).

1371. South Africa produces about ⅔ of the world's gold.

1372. If you pee in the shower instead of a toilet at least once a day you can save up to 2,000 liters of water every year.

1373. If a lion takes over the pride of lions, he kills the whole generation of the previous leader.

1374. Many of the famines of the past resulted not from a lack of food but from bad or deliberate government policies.

1375. The residents of Bougainville Island, located in the Pacific, speak Rotokas which includes only 12 letters; the alphabet is based on Latin and includes letters a, e, g, i, k, o, p, r, s, t, u, v.

1376. Siberian tiger is the biggest wildcat and can be as big as a small car.

1377. A glass ball will bounce higher than a rubber ball.

1378. You cannot commit suicide by holding your breath.

1379. Planet Saturn would float on water because its density is so low.

1380. More than 300,000 residents of Sweden have Carlson as their last name.

1381. Movie actresses look a lot better on the screen than in real life.

1382. The total damage caused by natural disasters between 2000 and 2012 is equivalent to $1.7 trillion and it affected 2.9 billion people.

1383. Snickers candy was named after the favorite horse of a confectioner.

1384. The rarest material on planet Earth is astatine. In all the Earth's crust, you can collect only 0.16 grams of it.

1385. The cats rub against people to leave their scent with the area with the scent glands around its face. It also has scent glands on the paws and tail.

1386. The largest ethnic group in the world that doesn't have a country is Kurdish.

1387. Facebook and YouTube are blocked in Syria.

1388. In Syria, a week begins with a Sunday.

1389. "French kiss" is known as the "English kiss" in France.

1390. There is more surface area in Russia than there is on Pluto.

1391. If you had $0.01 and double it every day you would become a millionaire after just 27 days.

1392. A tarantula will bite you if it is cornered, otherwise it prefers to run away.

1393. The bite of a tarantula is equivalent to the bite of a bee by its toxicity and consequences.

1394. If you concentrate on falling asleep, it will be even harder than if you didn't.

1395. Women have more pain receptors on the body, but they also have a higher pain tolerance.

1396. The word for school comes from ancient Greek for "free time".

1397. There are more stars in the sky than there are grains of sand in all the beaches of the world.

1398. You could survive for a month without the food, but only a week without the water.

1399. You feel thirst when the amount of water in your body drops by just one percent.

1400. A tarantula can grow back its limbs when it molts.

1401. The external chitinous skeleton of a tarantula is very fragile, so any fall can lead to a deadly trauma for the spider.

1402. Tarantulas can produce a web, but they never use it for hunting, instead they use it to cover the eggs and to insulate their nests.

1403. Tarantulas have claws at the end of the paws. The claws can come forward like in a cat. The claws help the spider crawl around all kinds of places.

1404. Thailand became a very popular tourist destination after the Vietnam War when the American soldiers rested here.

1405. Thai people didn't use the last names until 1913.

1406. Cats can run at a speed of 31 mph over a short distance.

1407. Unlike other countries in the South East Asia, Thailand has not been anyone's colony.

1408. The Siamese cats originated in Thailand.

1409. Khmer language, native to Cambodia, has the longest alphabet in the world.

1410. If you raise your voice in Thailand, you automatically lose the argument.

1411. You can get a driver's license in Thailand in half a day just by listening to a lecture about the driving rules and by taking a ride with an instructor.

1412. In Thai calendar, the year is 2,560.

1413. If somebody insults a king of Thailand, he can end up in prison even if he or she is a foreigner.

1414. The names of hurricanes are invented in an alphabetical order (Harvey, Irma, Jose, and Katia) for every year.

1415. The official nickname of Hawaii is the "Aloha state", or a hospitable state.

1416. Hawaii is the only state that has two official languages. Guess which ones? English and Hawaiian.

1417. For every human there are 1.6 million ants, but they weigh as much as all the humans.

1418. You can find snow in Hawaii, on top of the mountains.

1419. All the islands of Hawaii are located near active volcanoes.

1420. Killaway volcano began erupting in 1983 and it continue to erupt to this day.

1421. There is a house in Hawaii that is located on top of an active volcano.

1422. Hawaii has the highest life expectancy of all the states.

1423. The surface area in Hawaii slowly but continuously grows due to the constant volcanic eruptions.

1424. There are no snakes in Hawaii.

1425. In China you can get a fine if you damage the Great Wall.

1426. The cleanest sea in the world is in Antarctica.

1427. The Wall of China that is presented to the tourists is partially restored because the part of it was dismantled in the 20th century for construction materials.

1428. About 40 million tourists visit the Great Wall of China every year.

1429. The Great Wall of China is considered the biggest cemetery in the world because for its construction, between 400,000 and a million workers died there.

1430. There are rivers in Antarctica.

1431. It rains diamonds on Jupiter and Saturn.

1432. "Project Mars" was a book written in 1952 by Wernher von Braun which envisioned that human colonists on Mars would be led by a person called "Elon".

1433. The average width of the Great Wall of China is about six meters.

1434. During the Gold Rush in Alaska, potato was as valuable as gold. You could get a pound of potato for a pound of gold. Many people during the Gold Rush suffered from scurvy, and potatoes were a good remedy against it.

1435. One end of the Great Wall of China is located at the sea.

1436. The largest tsunami ever recorded happened in 1958 in Alaska when a large glacier fell into the lake creating a wave greater than half a kilometer in height.

1437. So far ten people were born in Antarctica.

1438. The length of the Great Wall of China is about 9 thousand kilometers, or almost 6 thousand miles.

1439. The largest earthquake in history occurred in Chili in the 1960s.

1440. You can synthesize water by burning rocket fuel.

1441. The Olympic flag has the colors of black, blue, green, and yellow rings because every nation in the world has a flag with one of these colors.

1442. The little paper flag that sticks out from the top of Hershey's kisses is called "Nigglywiggly".

1443. Crayola is derived from French, meaning oily chalk.

1444. A grizzly bear can crush a bowling ball with its bite.

1445. If you kill a Panda in China, you can be punished by death.

1446. Koalas have such a small brain that they cannot perform complex and unfamiliar tasks such as eating leaves on flat surfaces.

1447. Angora rabbit is the world's fluffiest bunny.

1448. Charlie Chaplin came third in a Charlie Chaplin lookalike contest which he entered anonymously.

1449. Class Seven authorization is a "license to kill" issued by the British Secret Service, and it must be approved by the MI6 agent's superiors all the way up to the Foreign Minister.

1450. There is a cat in Bridport, UK that regularly catches a bus to a nearby city. It happens so often that the drivers bring tin of cat food with them and know which stop to let him off at.

1451. Due to its granite construction, The Grand Central Station in New York is more radioactive than a nuclear power plant.

1452. Barbara Soper, a woman from Michigan gave birth on 10/10/10, 09/09/09 and 08/08/08. These are the odds of 50 million to one.

1453. After hurricane Katrina there was a reduction of 85 percent in the number of babies named Katrina.

1454. More than 7,000 people die every year due to a sloppy handwriting of doctors. Another 1.5 million American are injured every year and die to preventable medication mistakes.

1455. When asking for something, add "but you are free to refuse" at the end to double your chances of getting what you want.

1456. Nikola Tesla's teachers mistakenly thought that he was cheating because he could do integral calculus in his head.

1457. Some of the suggested names for Pixar's Toy Story was "Made in Taiwan, Moving Buddies, and Toyz in the Hood."

1458. The problem of overpopulation in 14th century Europe was solved by the Plague. As a result, wages increased, rent decreased, wealth was more evenly distributed, diet improved, and life expectancy increased.

1459. It is good for children's imagination to believe in Santa Claus and can be part of normal, healthy development.

1460. Psychopaths typically use too many "uhs" and "ums" when talking, to seem normal.

1461. $400,000 is the price of a single helmet for the Air Force's new F-35 fighter.

1462. Advertising by drug companies is illegal almost everywhere in the world but the US and New Zealand.

1463. In Palestine the divorce is banned during Ramadan because "people make hasty decisions when they are hungry".

1464. The most commonly used passwords in Microsoft devices include "123456," "password," "monkey," and "abcdefg." They are all being banned.

1465. Spiders eat between 400 and 800 million tons of insects and other pests each year.

1466. When the inheritance tax was abolished in Australia in 1979, a disproportionate number of parents died in the week immediately after the abolition went into effect. This suggests that many of their heirs were trying to keep them alive just long enough for the inheritance tax to expire.

1467. Costco does not have signs intentionally to keep customers walking through the aisles and find things to buy.

1468. In Africa there is a new Ocean being formed.

1469. Michael Jackson did not want his kids to see him drink alcohol, so he requested his wine to be served in Diet Coke cans during a flight.

1470. It is estimated that there are as many Russian spies in London as during the height of Cold War.

1471. In China there is a 1,300-year-old city submerged in a man-made lake.

1472. If you find a stranded dolphin on the shores, do not hurry to help it back into the water because most of the time dolphins come out intentionally when injured or sick to avoid drowning.

1473. “Percussive maintenance” means hitting something until it works.

1474. Before the invention of alarm clocks people used to drink lots of water before bed so that their over-full bladder would wake them up.

1475. North Korea has around 6-10 trillion dollars’ worth of minerals underground, but it cannot access it due to a lack of technology and equipment.

1476. Red hair and blue eyes is the rarest combination occurring in only 1 percent of the human population.

1477. It took 6.3 million tons of material to build the Great Pyramid. This is more material than it took to build all the churches and cathedrals in England.

1478. Samsung used to sell noodles before they started selling electronics in 1970.

1479. NASA was issued a $20 parking ticket for landing on an asteroid that was claimed by a man named Gregory Nemitz.

1480. Cheetahs make meowing sounds just like cats.

1481. In the past 1000 years Icelandic language has barely changed. Because of this, school children can read texts written in the 12th century.

1482. Unexplored passageways still exist in the Great Pyramid of Giza.

1483. The oldest message in a bottle spent 97 years and 309 days at sea and was found in Scotland in 2012.

1484. There was a major accident on a highway due to somebody stopping in the middle of the lane to allow a family of ducks to cross unharmed.

1485. There are cities in Russia which are completely closed to the foreign visitors. There are 44 of them and there are 1.5 million people.

1486. When men listen to women's voices, it activates the same part of the brain that processes the sound of music.

1487. Prolonged, unnatural smiling can lead to a Smile Mask Syndrome in which a person has depression and a physical illness.

1488. Ultra-pure water can kill you because it can take out minerals from your body if drank enough.

1489. The most popular pet in North America is a cat. There are 73 million cats compared to 63 million dogs. About 30 percent of households own a cat.

1490. Just like adults talking, the babies have accents when they cry. A French baby's cry will end with a rising note, while a German baby has a dropping note at the end. They pick it up in the womb.

1491. 62 percent of people tell an average of 2-3 lies every minute; 91 percent of people lie regularly both at work and at home.

1492. Doctors in British Columbia are forbidden to talk about hockey during surgery.

1493. "Ninja lanternshark" is a newly discovered shark which has a jet-black body and a glowing head.

1494. Buckminster Fuller was an inventor and an architect who tried to document his life as completely as possible. He recorded his diary every 15 minutes from 1915 to 1983. His diary is known as 'Dymaxion Chronofile'. It contains 14,000 papers and is a staggering 82 meters high.

1495. Myfridgefood.com lets you enter whatever ingredients you have in your fridge and tells you what recipes you can make with them.

1496. In an interview Elon Musk stated that he "wants to die on Mars, just not on impact."

1497. In 1989, Bill Gates answered a Microsoft tech support call, and identified himself only as "William", then solved the issue. The customer called back later specifically requesting him.

1498. One of the New York Mafia families' rules is that the members aren't allowed to grow facial hair.

1499. Launching a nuclear weapon in the City of Chicago is punishable by a $1,000 fine.

1500. There are only 2 gun-related homicides per year in Japan.

1501. Cheating and creating cheats for online games is officially a crime in South Korea.

1502. Each button on an Xbox controller can withstand 3 million presses.

1503. A Tetris Syndrome is when you play a game for too long and then you start to dream and hallucinate about it.

1504. The first democratically elected woman to lead a state was from Iceland and she was the president from 1980 to 1996.

1505. Aztec mothers who died in childbirth were regarded as highly as warriors who died in battle.

1506. There is a bar in Tokyo where you can have a drink with penguins.

1507. It is not allowed to fly over the White House and Disneyland. You will be intercepted by fighter jets.

1508. Your dog will use deception to get a tasty treat from you.

1509. Cats that do not bury their poop are telling you that they are in charge.

1510. The brain of the dog releases oxytocin when it sees its owner, it is the same chemical found in humans who are in love or bonding with friends.

1511. If helium is cooled to near absolute zero it becomes a liquid that flows against gravity.

1512. One British prisoner of WWI was released by the Germans so he could visit his dying mother, and then returned as he had made promise to the Kaiser Wilhelm II.

1513. According to a 2009 OkCupid statistics, women rate 80 percent of men "below average".

1514. Cheerios sends out 500 free wildflower seeds when you sign up on their website, which can be planted to create more bee habitat.

1515. When a baby is born in Korea, it automatically becomes one year old, and their age increases on New Year's which is Dec. 31st.

1516. A British scientist decided to perform an experiment where he rode a bike on the road to see how much distance the passing cars would give him. He found that drivers gave him 6 more inches when he was wearing a wig.

1517. In 1977 a Chinese woman with no medical degree anonymously discovered a cure for malaria. 38 years later, she was awarded the Nobel prize for medicine.

1518. 350 years ago, Robert Boyle wrote down a 'to-do list' of fantastical things he hoped science would one day accomplish. We are over halfway there.

1519. People who have a Fregoli delusion think that everyone they meet is the same person in disguise.

1520. The reason why your face turns red during anger is because your heart beats faster to send more blood to the muscles and prepare you for the fight.

1521. Of all the people that ever existed on planet Earth 93 percent are dead and about 50 percent of them were killed by malaria.

1522. Most serial killers have been born in November than any other month.

1523. Rene' Laennec was a highly religious physician who invented a stethoscope because he was uncomfortable putting his ear to the chest of women.

1524. The doctor that discovered that washing hands helps prevent the spread of diseases was thrown into a mental institution for crazy people.

1525. El Salvador and Honduras declared war at each other over a soccer game in 1969 that lasted 100 hours.

1526. If a car is moving five miles per hour slower than traffic it has a greater chance of causing an accident than a car moving 5 hours faster than traffic.

1527. The assassin of President James A. Garfield intentionally used a gun that would look nice in a museum.

1528. Sometimes pandas prefer to sit alone when they are sad.

1529. Three Scottish soldiers escaped capture from the German soldiers when they spoke their native Gaelic to confuse them after their capture claiming they were Ukrainian. Therefore, German soldiers let them go.

1530. Kurt Cobain worked as a janitor in a high school after dropping out from that same high school.

1531. If order to prevent further suicides on a South Korea's Mapo Bridge, it was renamed the Bridge of Life, decorated with positive affirmations and even sympathetic sculptures. Suicides increased six-fold the following year.

1532. Crocodiles, Alligators and Flounders have no finite life span, but continue to live forever unless affected by their environment.

1533. Cats were condemned as evil by Pope Innocent VIII during the Spanish Inquisition. This lead to the burning of thousands of cats. As a result, rat population exploded leading to more severe effects of the Plague.

1534. One of Rio's $12 billion Olympic parks is mostly abandoned and off limits to tourism.

1535. There are enough diamonds in existence to give everyone on the planet a cupful.

1536. A German passport grants a visa-free access to 177 countries out of 218.

1537. There are 100 times more chances to be bit by another human in New York City than to be bit by a shark at the beach.

1538. Tetraphobia is very common among Asians. It is a fear of number four. Asians are more likely to die of a heart attack on the 4th of a month than any other day of the month.

1539. James Holmes, the man behind the Colorado movie theater mass shooting in 2012 was sentenced to 3,318 years in prison.

1540. In fifth grade, future "Friends" actor Matthew Perry and a friend beat up future Canadian prime minister Justin Trudeau.

1541. One of the oldest statues in Bern, Switzerland is of a man eating babies, and nobody really knows why it's there.

1542. Bananas are a natural sleep aid because they contain melatonin, which helps regulate the body's natural rhythms.

1543. The doctor who popularized the idea of "Alpha" and "Beta" members of wolf packs has spent the rest of his career trying to convince everyone he was wrong.

1544. Solastalgia is the term for feeling uneasy or distressed when the landscape or natural environment around your home is changing for the worse, and there's nothing you can do to stop it.

1545. If you are constantly dreaming about your high-stress job, don't worry - your brain is just learning how to do that job better.

1546. In Japan, '39' is a common text speak for 'thank you', due to how 3 (san) and 9 (kyu) sound when spoken out loud.

1547. The "greenest" country in the world is Iceland because it uses 100 percent of renewable energy.

1548. Swansea Jack was a black retriever that lived in Newfoundland, Canada, in the 1930's. In seven years of his lifetime the dog was able to rescue an estimated 27 people from drowning. He was named 'Dog of the Century' in 2000.

1549. An old card table bought for $25 at a garage sale turned out to be one of 6 tables left in the world by furniture makers John Seymour & Son. It later sold for $541,000 at an auction.

1550. A war between Switzerland and Liechtenstein almost started several times, but not because of tensions and disagreements but because of accidents. In 1985 Swiss army accidentally bombed Liechtenstein during a drill. In 1992 they accidentally 'invaded' their neighbor while setting up an observation post. And in 2007 Swiss soldiers lost their way and crossed the border. A spokesman of Liechtenstein simply said, "No problem, these things happen".

1551. Your eyes adjust to the dark in 15 to 20 minutes, it's about the same time it takes for the sun to set.

1552. Taking written notes means you understand material much better than somebody who types them on a computer.

1553. Intelligent people are more likely to trust others.

1554. "Iceberg Mansions" are homes that are mostly underground, and they are being built by billionaires in London.

1555. The oldest known pet cat was found in the Mediterranean on an island of Cyprus 9,500 years old.

1556. Most of Steve Jobs' wealth was from his shares in Disney, not Apple.

1557. Sara Breedlove became the first woman millionaire in the 1890's by selling hair products designed and marketed for black women.

1558. Napoleon's brother, Louis Bonaparte, was known as The King of Rabbits because he mispronounced the Dutch phrase "I am your king" and instead said "I am your rabbit" when he took over the Netherlands in 1806.

1559. Studies show that anxiety and intelligence coevolved, so if you are highly anxious you might also have a higher IQ than people who are not anxious.

1560. In Swedish capital, Stockholm, good drivers can win a lottery paid with the money from bad drivers for fines.

1561. The 2022 World Cup Final will be played in Lusail, Qatar, a city that does not exist yet.

1562. Pakistani passports have an inscription "This passport is valid for all countries of the World except Israel."

1563. In Japan, Hiroshima Peace Flame has been burning continuously since it was lit in 1964; it will remain lit until all nuclear bombs on the planet are destroyed and the planet is free from the threat of nuclear annihilation.

1564. President Jefferson postponed a state dinner for the Tunisian ambassador until after sunset to accommodate the ambassador's observance of the Ramadan fast, in 1805.

1565. Geothermal heat in Iceland is used by the locals to bake bread in the ground buried in pots.

1566. In the summer of 1790 George Washington spent $200 on ice cream which in today's money is equivalent to $5,100.

1567. In WWII, Hershey produced a chocolate bar for American soldiers and it was meant to taste so bad that the soldiers would eat it only when they starved.

1568. A man survived the sinking of a ship in 1871, leaving him traumatized afterwards. Some forty years later he was finally able to overcome his fears and sail again… only to die on the Titanic.

1569. The sheep in New Zealand outnumber the people six to one.

1570. In Amsterdam alcoholics were hired to pick up trash and they were paid in beer.

1571. Symptoms of psychiatric disorders such as depression are visible in PhD students twice as much as in other people.

1572. In Australia 20,000-year-old fossilized human footprints were discovered indicating that the person who made them was running at a speed of a modern Olympic sprinter, barefoot, in sand.

1573. Genetically you are more like your dad than your mom.

1574. Usain Bolt turned down all the scholarships from American colleges to train in Jamaica.

1575. D-IX was a Nazi experimental cocktail that allowed soldiers to walk 55 miles without resting.

1576. In the Victorian Era people used rocking bathtubs to recreate the waves of an ocean at home.

1577. Queen of England uses her handbag to send secret signals to her staff when she needs help getting out of a conversation with someone.

1578. Harry Whittington was shot in the face by Dick Cheney during a hunting accident. He revealed in 2010 that Cheney has neither publicly nor privately apologized to Whittington for the shooting.

1579. Nutella has very few hazelnuts and is 58 percent sugar and 32 percent fat, most of which is palm oil.

1580. You can smell someone's fear through chemical pheromones released through their sweat.

1581. A coat can be made of 24 cat skins

1582. Arctic Fox is the only mammal native to Iceland.

1583. Dogs that are small, elderly or short-haired need sweaters for cold weather.

1584. At age 25 Julius Caesar was kidnapped by pirates. He told them he would kill them when he was free, and he kept his promise.

1585. Some of the shooting stars we can see from Earth are astronaut poop burning up in the atmosphere.

1586. In 2011, a pair of managers from Dominos set fire to a Papa John's to boost their sales.

1587. In 2012, the world's first lab grown burger cost $325,000. By 2015, a lab grown burger only cost $11.36.

1588. People are more likely to regret things that they haven't done than the things that they have done.

1589. Thioacetone is a chemical that smells so bad that a small, test tube amount, can cause nausea half a mile away.

1590. The "6" in SEAL Team 6 was added to throw off the Russians during Cold War. It was meant to make the Russian intelligence think that five more teams of equal caliber were deployed.

1591. The fresh, salty smell of beach air is the smell of rotting seaweed.

1592. In Spain, pork is popular because it was used to show that you are not a Jew or Muslim during the Inquisition.

1593. There are just as many ship and plane disappearances in the Bermuda Triangle as any other region of the ocean.

1594. To spread awareness and to prove to everyone that snakes do not bite unless provoked, a man in India spent 72 hours in a cage with 72 of the most venomous snake species in India. He came out of the cage unharmed without a single bite.

1595. The modern office chair with its wheels was created by Charles Darwin.

1596. A group of flies is called a business.

1597. "Afghanistanism" means the practice of concentrating on problems in distant parts of the world while ignoring controversial local issues. This term is almost 70 years old.

1598. People in poorer countries are more likely to say they are having a good day than people in affluent countries.

1599. 'Analysis paralysis' is when you can't decide because you've overanalyzed the pros and cons to the point that you're too overwhelmed to come to a rational conclusion and therefore fail to make any decision at all.

1600. Octopuses are given puzzles in captivity so that they don't get bored and because they are so smart.

1601. It has been observed that ravens can call wolves to the site of the dead animals so that they will open the carcass and leave the scraps more accessible to them.

1602. It is common for people in Japan to peel the grapes because it is too dirty or too bitter.

1603. Lack of sleep for a period of 3 to 5 years can shrink your brain.

1604. When Pablo Picasso was asked about the meaning of his paintings he would take out a revolver from his pocket and shoot at people with the blank bullets.

1605. On Mars, without a spacesuit, you would pass out in 30 seconds and be dead in 1 minute.

1606. Nearly four million cats are eaten in Asia every day.

1607. Before becoming successful, Walt Disney had to eat dog food to survive.

1608. The secret service of the United States has its own flag.

1609. Adults who need glasses create a $227 billion dollar fall in economy due to a loss in productivity.

1610. "Fremdscham" is a German word for being embarrassed for someone else.

1611. Sony makes more money in Japan as an insurance company than selling the electronics.

1612. The Lord of the Rings was originally published as one massive book, not a trilogy.

1613. If a potato is exposed to light while growing it will become green and poisonous.

1614. Netherlands surrendered to Nazi Germany in just 5 days.

1615. Sexually transmitted disease can affect plants too.

1616. It takes up to 200 days for a leech to digest food.

1617. The Chinese invasion of Taiwan in 1949 was prevented by a river snail and a parasite.

1618. There are more than 400 words and expressions for word 'snow' in Scotland.

1619. If you are one of those people who enjoy being alone and single while waiting for the right person instead of dating casually than the best word to describe you is 'Quirkyalone'.

1620. According to a study, astrologers are no better at determining people's psychological traits based on the location of the stars during their birth than someone who is randomly guessing them.

1621. Rats are more efficient at detecting mines than the electronic minesweepers and with higher accuracy.

1622. The cost of a pack of cigarettes in Australia will increase to $40 by 2020.

1623. The longest lasting emotion is sadness which can take around 4 days to pass.

1624. You can die from staying awake for 2 weeks straight.

1625. Russians used to think that the Jews eat some secret vegetable that prevents them from becoming alcoholics. Anti-Semitism was justified because the Jews refused to share their magic vegetable.

1626. Beating up your dog in South Carolina leads to a more severe sentence than for beating up your wife.

1627. 35 restaurants in China were under investigation for putting opium poppy into food to get customers hooked.

1628. Cats can make about 100 different sounds whereas the dogs can make only 10.

1629. If you are a person who reads in bed than you are a librocubicularist.

1630. 'Companion' is a Latin word meaning 'someone with whom you share bread'.

1631. If an ant encounters a drunk comrade, it will carry him home to sleep it off.

1632. Your heart will pump enough blood in a lifetime to fill three supertankers.

1633. American Presidents George Washington, Thomas Jefferson, Andrew Jackson, Martin Van Buren, and Dwight Eisenhower all had red hair.

1634. Dogs have evolved to understand human laughter due to a long historical bond.

1635. Pupils can expand up to 45 percent when looking at someone you love.

1636. Two years after retirement, 78 percent of former NFL players are broke or under financial stress. Five years after retirement, 60 percent of former NBA players are broke.

1637. A big part of "Game of Thrones" was filmed in Iceland.

1638. In Japan, Kyoto means "capital city", and it was a former capital. Tokyo means "eastern capital".

1639. Making a phone call from a prison is very expensive. Companies who charge for the calls make $1.2 billion per year.

1640. Eating fish at least once a week leads to thicker, stronger and more resilient brains.

1641. Despite being free for use by the world, the operating cost of GPS is $2 million a day.

1642. Camels were originally adapted to the arctic and not the desert.

1643. First born children tend to have a higher IQ than their siblings.

1644. Up to 5 million tweets are read by the CIA every day.

1645. A "tramp" is someone who only works when they are forced to, a "bum" doesn't work at all, and a "hobo" is a traveling worker.

1646. Iceland is known as the "land of fire and ice" because it has many active volcanoes among its glaciers.

1647. Six different nations governed Texas: Spain, France, Mexico, the Republic of Texas, the United States, and the Confederate States of America. Hence the name "Six Flags".

1648. Coca-Cola used to contain about nine milligrams of cocaine in each glass.

1649. Women are more attracted to men with a sense of humor because humor is associated with intelligence and honesty.

1650. When you talk to someone and the person starts to blink rapidly it means that their mind is wandering and not paying attention.

1651. During a sunburn, it is not your skin being damaged, but the skin's DNA being damaged and killing the skin cells so they do not turn into cancer cells.

1652. The fear of being or falling in love is known as philophobia.

1653. In 1998 there were 300,000 African lions, but only 23,000 are left now.

1654. A space suit costs around one million dollars and takes about 5,000 hours to make.

1655. CNN once had two reporters talk to each other via satellite while they were standing in the same parking lot.

1656. Sushi appeared 2000 years ago, not in Japan, but Southeast Asia along the Mekong River. It later spread out to other regions and reached Japan in 8th century AD.

1657. A group of cats is called a "clowder".

1658. 2010 was the last payment that Germany made for the damages caused during World War I.

1659. Cristoforo Colombo is the real name of an Anglicized Christopher Columbus.

1660. When the Hobbit movie was in the process of making, the film crew used up all the gold paint for Smaug's Lair. They had to import more from Germany.

1661. The Da Vinci Code was denounced by the Catholic Church making it more popular.

1662. Iceland is the only NATO country without a standing army.

1663. Gaius Appuleius Diocles was the highest paid athlete of all time. He was a Roman Charioteer. In today's money he earned about $15 billion in prize money alone.

1664. If you kill an elephant in Sri Lanka, you will be punished with death.

1665. Eight-year-old Gabi Mann receives gifts from crows in her garden for feeding them. Some of the gifts include a miniature silver ball, a black button, a blue paper clip, a yellow bead, a blue Lego piece, and a pearl colored heart.

1666. Originally the pyramids of Egypt were white and smooth as they were encased in marble.

1667. Semen was used as an invisible ink by the British spies during WWI; it was invented by Sir Mansfield Cumming.

1668. The rarest type of blonde hair is strawberry blonde.

1669. Students at Christ's Hospital Boarding School in England have been wearing the same uniform since 1556.

1670. BLA Frank Calder was defeated by one vote during the 1979 British Columbia election. He later admitted that he and his wife had neglected to vote.

1671. It is common for the residents of Churchill, Manitoba to leave their car doors unlocked in case somebody will need a shelter from a polar bear.

1672. There were many attempts to assassinate Hitler. 26 known attempts from 1934 to 1944, four attempts before 1933, and 10 attempts from 1933 to 1934. Almost all of them were carried out by German citizens.

1673. According to research, laziness is a normal part of being a teenager and does not reflect bad behavior.

1674. During World War II people of German heritage were suspect in the US. There were protests against ethnic

Germans which included violence such as burning of German books, killing of German shepherds, and even the killing of one German American.

1675. On average, people that complain live longer because it helps release tension which, in turn, strengthens the immune system and boosts the health.

1676. Mortgage translates as "death pledge" into modern English. Mort - from the French meaning "Death" and Gage - from Old English meaning "Pledge".

1677. There are no mosquitoes in Iceland.

1678. Female dragonflies fake their death sometimes to avoid having sex.

1679. Canada has been ranked number one when it comes to 'quality of life' for the second year in a row in 2017.

1680. In the months following the 9/11 about 1,000 deaths occurred because Americans chose to travel by car instead of by plane.

1681. Being lonely can damage you both physically and mentally.

1682. There are 3G mobile services on Mount Everest so that you could Tweet your ascent on the way to the summit.

1683. Decades ago, you had 17 minutes to escape the fire in the house before everything goes up in flames. Now you only have 3 minutes because the synthetic materials in our homes burn up faster than the natural products present in 70s and 80s.

1684. In the world's quietest room, you can hear your own blood flowing.

1685. The USPS Mail Delivery Vehicles are 25-30 years old & use engines designed in the 70s that get 10 MPG.

1686. Elephants are compassionate towards the weak and altruistic towards other species.

1687. Hypnic jerk has been experienced by up to 70 percent of people. It is a falling sensation that wakes you up suddenly as you are almost asleep.

1688. 84 percent of vegans and vegetarians eventually go back to eating meat.

1689. In the 1960's, Iraq was named "one of the best countries to be a child" by UNICEF.

1690. Feeling tired even after a good night's sleep could be a sign of dehydration. Drinking water can help wake you up.

1691. Someone who hates everyone and everything is known as a misomaniac.

1692. Marmosets teach their offspring not to interrupt in conversation.

1693. Every ten years a new species of owl is discovered.

1694. Days on Venus are longer than its years because of how slowly it rotates on its axis.

1695. It is possible to think that you just awoke when you are still in deep sleep. It is known as a "False awakening".

1696. Bananas are a natural cure to reduce the effects of stress and anxiety.

1697. All the photos of the Milky Way that you see are not of our actual galaxy. They are the photos of another spiral galaxy known as Messier 74. Our galaxy is 100,000 years across and we are stuck inside.

1698. The former president of Liberia Charles King won the presidential elections in 1927 with 234,000 votes in a country of 15,000 voters placing him in a Guinness World record for the most fraudulent election.

1699. Treating balance problems during childhood can help reduce anxiety and boost self-esteem.

1700. Crows (and other corvids) can remember individual human faces, hold grudges against us, and teach their crow brothers and sisters to dislike us too.

1701. When we burn fat during an exercise, the 'lost weight' is exhaled as carbon dioxide and water.

1702. The shortest international bridge in the world is between Portugal and Spain.

1703. While filming Return of the Jedi in the forests of the Pacific Northwest, actor Peter Mayhew, who is 7'2", was given strict instructions to never wander off in his Chewbacca costume so that he wouldn't get shot by somebody mistaking him for Bigfoot.

1704. Some of the products used by McDonald's, Starbucks, Victoria's Secret and Boeing are made by prisoners.

1705. In 1954 a democratically elected president has been deposed by the CIA and replaced by a dictator to save investments in a banana company.

1706. One man, named James Howells, threw away a hard drive containing 7,500 bitcoins. The hard drive is currently under mountains of trash in a Wales landfill and it is worth $15 million.

1707. A nuclear missile crewman, Harold Hering, was kicked out of the military for asking "How can I know that an order to launch my missiles came from a sane president?"

1708. Our sense of taste decreases by 20% to 50% when we are flying.

1709. Your fingerprint is not protected under the 5th amendment, so police can force you to unlock a phone with a fingerprint but not a password.

1710. In India all doctors are required by law to write prescriptions in CAPITAL LETTERS in a 'Legible' writing as a measure to prevent deaths caused by the misinterpretation of their sloppy handwriting.

1711. In 2014, a British sniper in Afghanistan killed six insurgents with a single bullet after hitting the trigger switch of a suicide bomber whose device then exploded.

1712. Doing things that scare you will make you happier.

1713. Coffee is most effective if consumed between 9:30 am and 11:30 am.

1714. Amazon ships bubble wrap in bubble wrap.

1715. All presidents and first ladies have secret service protection for life, and any children of former president get secret service protection until they turn 16.

1716. There are more calories in a McDonald's Caesar Salad than the Double Big Mac Burger.

1717. In WWI dogs were used as messengers to carry orders to the front lines.

1718. Queen ants are one of the longest living insects and can live over 30 years.

1719. We are used to seeing Bugs Bunny eating carrots, but this is misleading because rabbit's natural diet does not include roots, fruits, or iceberg lettuce.

1720. About 80 percent of jobs in the US have never been posted or advertised.

1721. There have been more than 17,000 British and American children who auditioned for the role of Harry Potter.

1722. One time a man staged his kidnapping in front of his wife so he could go and party all night long with his friends.

1723. Two million cases of diabetes could be prevented by 2020 if Americans stopped drinking soda every day.

1724. A 300-page book called 'A Void' has been written without using letter 'e'. The original book is in French and it has been translated into other languages that also avoided using the most common letter in the alphabet.

1725. There was a cat named Toldo who visited his dead owner's grave for over a year. Every time the cat brought a small gift that included leaves, sticks, twigs, plastic cups, or paper towels.

1726. Saddam Hussein was given a key to the city of Detroit in 1980 because of his donations to local churches.

1727. When multilingual people switch a language they also switch their personality.

1728. The probability of a road rage increases the more bumper stickers there are on the car.

1729. The police records of people in Florida are always public and can show up on the news.

1730. A policeman from South Africa, Andre Stander, used to rob banks on his lunch break and often returned as an investigating officer.

1731. In Vietnam, the Vietnam War is known as the American War.

1732. The people who were voicing Mickey and Minnie Mouse got married in real life.

1733. In recent years, dozens of North Korean "ghost ships", many containing corpses, have washed up on the Japanese coast.

1734. "Fake guest" agencies exist in South Korea because the number of guests at the wedding is so important.

1735. Moscow is home to the most skyscrapers in Europe.

1736. The Sandbox Tree is covered in spikes that contain poison and it grows exploding fruits for which it is known as a Dynamite Tree.

1737. In WWII, the US considered dying Mt. Fuji in black as a psychological warfare against Japan.

1738. The red panda has no close relatives and it is the only living species in its genus and family.

1739. Badgers and coyotes hunt together. A badger digs up the prey and the coyote runs it down.

1740. Cats and killer whales both kill for fun.

1741. In 1860, Abraham Lincoln found out that his new biography mistakenly mentioned a book that he supposedly read - so he made sure to read that book to keep the integrity.

1742. There is a fish that can induce hallucinations like LSD if eaten. In Hawaii the effects are known as "the chief of ghosts" and in Arabic as "the fish that makes dreams".

1743. Lenin didn't trust Stalin and wanted him to be removed from power because Lenin was "not sure if he can be trusted to use authority with sufficient caution".

1744. It is legal to smash someone's car window to save a pet from overheating in Florida.

1745. United Airlines is offering up to $10,000 to passengers who give up seats on overbooked flights.

1746. The average American thinks that he or she is smarter than the average American.

1747. According to a study from the London School of Economics and Political Sciences our joy in life peaks at two ages - 23 and 69.

1748. Raccoons did not inhabit Japan until 1977, the year when a popular anime caused many people to import them as pets, some of which escaped into the wild.

1749. Some coyotes in the US have figured out how traffic lights work and use them to cross the road safely.

1750. In Arizona, there is a town called Nothing, with a population of 0. Nothing once contained a gas station and a small convenience store.

1751. Adolf Hitler wanted to be a priest when he was a child.

1752. Hundreds of archaeology professors and students were inspired by Indiana Jones: Raiders of the Lost Ark, after which the number of students in archaeology increased.

1753. There is a variation of soccer where 3 teams meet each other at the same time.

1754. Due to a superstition, there are ravens that are enlisted as soldiers in the United Kingdom. They are always kept at the Tower of London. They have been occasionally dismissed for bad conduct. While wild ravens live for 10-15 years, Tower ravens can live past 40 years.

1755. A newly hatched baby chick is smarter than a newborn baby human.

1756. The average inmate at Alcatraz read 75-100 books per year.

1757. There is enough uranium in the ocean to power the planet for 10,000 years.

1758. Japan only has a military for defense, which means they cannot go out of the country to fight somewhere else.

1759. People who turn 100 years old in the US receive a letter from the President congratulating them on their longevity.

1760. Grafting is a process of splicing trees together by hand, which allows trees to grow multiple kinds of fruit on the same tree. These trees are called 'fruit salad trees.'

1761. There are 27 times more deaths caused by motorcycles per mile traveled than by cars.

1762. For chicken to be "free range," it must have access to the outdoors for a minimum of five minutes per day.

1763. There are red bananas that taste sweet, creamy, and a little bit like raspberries.

1764. Hitler and Nazi officials outlawed animal cruelty including the boiling of live lobsters.

1765. Many of the restaurant food poisonings occur due to uncleaned ice machines, not actual food.

1766. In 1971 scientists lit a hole filled with natural gas on fire expecting the hole to burn for a few days; the hole has been burning for the past 40 years. It is known as "The Door to Hell."

1767. Pope John Paul II was shot four times by a Turkish man in 1981. After his recovery, the Pope visited the assassin in the prison and forgave him. The assassin was pardoned at the Pope's request and 33 years after his crime, he visited Vatican City and laid flowers on the Pope's tomb.

1768. After the assassination of John F. Kennedy in 1963, Martin Luther King Jr. said to his wife, "this is what is going to happen to me also. I keep telling you, this is a sick society."

1769. Ravens can speak better than parrots, enjoy playing in the snow, make their own toys, and do weird things with ants.

1770. If the earth was the size of a billiard ball, the surface of the earth would be smoother than the ball's surface.

1771. Termites are planet's one of the most efficient bioreactors because they can produce up to 2 liters of hydrogen from ingesting a single sheet of paper.

1772. About half of all the pigs in the world are in China.

1773. 92 percent of the world's currency is in a digital format.

1774. "Esposas" in Spanish means both "handcuffs" and "wives" and it is not a coincidence.

1775. The reason why you can't remember anything after being drunk is because you were not creating memories in the first place.

1776. Every 64 days, your eyebrows renew themselves.

1777. Antibiotic resistance could become a more serious problem than cancer, leading to 10 million deaths per year.

1778. According to a Yale study, Crayola crayons are the third most recognizable scent, after coffee and peanut butter.

1779. Naked mole rats can tolerate acid, live 6 times longer than other rodents, survive long periods of oxygen deprivation and can live in heavily polluted areas. They were also forced to live in areas with high concentration of radiation and were injected carcinogens, but they never developed cancer.

1780. Ugly people are likelier to get harsher prison sentences as opposed to attractive people.

1781. There are no reliable studies to prove the health benefits of flossing, so it was dropped from the US government's dietary guidelines.

1782. The same temperature was observed in Antarctica and Cairo on March 1st, 2017; it was 63.5 degrees Fahrenheit, or 17.5 Celsius.

1783. 'Goth Chicken' is an extremely rare breed of chickens that resides in Indonesia. Their real name is the Ayam Cemani breed and they are entirely black from their feathers, beaks, and tongues, to their meat, bones, and internal organs.

1784. There are 20 bank robberies every day.

1785. The "Demon Duck of Doom," is an extinct type of a flightless bird that used to roam Australia. It was 8 ft tall and had a skull larger than that of some horses. Despite its name it was more related to modern chickens.

1786. There is a man who lives close to an airport in Milwaukee. He wrote on his roof, "Welcome to Cleveland", to confuse the passengers of the airplanes.

1787. No wars were permitted in the month before the ancient Olympics so that spectators could travel across Greece unharmed.

1788. Biological warfare could be traced back as early as the Mongol invasions when the Mongols would catapult the dead bodies of soldiers infected with the bubonic plague over city walls during sieges.

1789. According to a new research, on average, working over 39 hours a week leads to a decline in mental health, as there's less time for self-care.

1790. St. Valentine is the patron saint of love and marriage, but he was also a patron of beekeeping, epilepsy, fainting, and the plague.

1791. The Queen of Britain owns all whales and dolphins in the UK waters, due to a law dating from 1324, and all swans in the Thames.

1792. Many passages in the Old Testament, New Testament, and the Qur'an denounce and prohibit collecting interest on loans.

1793. Elephants can distinguish between human languages and can tell which languages have a history of hurting elephants.

1794. In Japan it is the women who give gifts to men on Valentine's Day, then on White Day, March 14th, it is the men who give the gifts to women.

1795. When you crack your knuckles, it does not hurt your bones or cause arthritis, the sound you hear is just gas bubbles bursting.

1796. According to studies acknowledging the awkwardness of an awkward silence is the fastest way to diffuse it.

1797. San Francisco became the first city in the United States to offer free community college to its residents, regardless of income.

1798. When you are sad, the perception of taste alters. Foods that you do not prefer taste even worse when you are upset. 'Comfort food' is what our subconscious mind wants so that the temporary sorrow doesn't ruin the taste.

1799. Only female mosquitoes drink blood, the males are vegetarians.

1800. Adolf Hitler's nephew, William fought for the US against his uncle in WWII.

1801. Benjamin Franklin wasn't trusted to write the Declaration of Independence because his peers feared he would include a joke in it.

1802. When you were just born, you held a record for being the "Youngest Person on The Planet."

1803. Popsicles were invented by accident by an 11-year old in 1905.

1804. There is a new app called Hater that matches people based on things that they mutually dislike.

1805. The world's oldest dress is 5,000 years old and it was found in Egypt.

1806. Stephen Hawking can choose to have a more "modernized" voice, but he chooses to keep the robotic voice as it is the voice he has come to identify with.

1807. There was a scientist that injected human brain cells into the head of a mouse, as a result, the mouse's memory and the ability to learn improved.

1808. Your brain blocks your vision every time when you are moving your eyes so that your life doesn't feel like a movie that's filmed with a shaky, handheld camera; this makes you completely blind for about 40 minutes a day.

1809. The Red Bull was created in Thailand in 1976 as an energy drink for truck drivers.

1810. Charles Darwin ate every animal that he discovered.

1811. The final words of Karl Marx were "Last words are for fools who haven't said enough!"

1812. If you want to have a full effect of fluoride in the toothpaste, do not rinse out your mouth after brushing your teeth.

1813. To find chimpanzees in the forest, the scientists often follow the sound of farts because chimpanzees fart loudly and frequently.

1814. If you marry your best friend, the risk of divorce is eliminated by 70 percent and the marriage is more likely to last a lifetime.

1815. HMS Artful is a British submarine that can stay submerged for 25 years without having to surface for air.

1816. One time a burglar was caught because he used the computer of the home that he robbed to log in to his Facebook account. The homeowner returned to find that the account was still logged in.

1817. To honor the funeral of Alexander Graham Bell all the telephone service in the US and Canada was silenced for one minute on August 4th, 1922.

1818. Calexico is a town on the California side of the US-Mexico border, and Mexicali is a town on the opposite side of the border.

1819. By the time he passed away in 1982, King Sobhuza II of Swaziland had 100 wives and more than 600 children.

1820. "Frequency illusion," also known as Baader-Meinhof phenomenon, is when a concept or thing you just found out about suddenly seems to appear everywhere.

1821. An exercise wheel was placed by researchers in the wild and it was used extensively by mice without any reward for using it. Other users included rats, shrews, and slugs.

1822. After being shown the atrocities of Holocaust many German soldiers of American POW burned their German uniforms.

1823. In Michigan, the recycle rate of plastic bottles is higher than any other states, at 97 percent, because a bottle deposit costs 10 cents compared to the usual 5 cents. Other states with bottle deposit laws have a 70 percent, and states without any deposit laws are at 33 percent.

1824. It is illegal for the teacher to keep the class after the bell as punishment because it violates the Geneva Convention's laws on collective punishment.

1825. Oak trees are struck by lightning more frequently than any other tree.

1826. You will be able to witness the collision of two stars in 2022.

1827. It cost the United States about the same amount of time and money to send a man to the moon and to find Osama Bin Laden.

1828. Pronoia is opposite of paranoia and it is a delusion that everyone is secretly plotting your success.

1829. Julius Caesar and Cleopatra had a child together whose name was Caesarion which translates to “Little Caesar”.

1830. Muhammad Ali saved 15 Americans from Iraq hostage by negotiating with Saddam Hussein all by himself.

1831. There is an 85-year old philanthropist Charles F. Feeney who has given away $8 billion throughout his lifetime and now has $2 million left to live on.

1832. Brazilian soccer star Ronaldinho first gained media attention when he was just 13 after his team won a game 23-0 and he scored all 23.

1833. If you fake a laugh for a very long time, you will start to really laugh, really hard.

1834. Macaques in Japan use coins to buy vending machine snacks.

1835. The blood from a horseshoe crab is bright blue, costs $15,000 per liter and has saved millions of lives.

1836. There are no spiders in Antarctica.

1837. If twin men had children with twin women, the offsprings would all be siblings genetically.

1838. There is a volcano in Tanzania that if you fall in its lava you can still survive because the lava is so cold that sometimes it freezes in midair.

1839. The private school that Bill Gates attended was the only school with a computer in all the US.

1840. There are enough saunas in Finland to have all the Finns take a sauna at the same time.

1841. The facial recognition algorithms used by Facebook outperforms those used by the FBI.

1842. Northern Sudanese desert has more pyramids than the entire country of Egypt.

1843. Coffee is the world's second most valuable traded commodity behind oil.

1844. Heart cancer is extremely rare because there is very little cell division as opposed to cell growth.

1845. The Apollo 11 astronauts have a moon on the Hollywood Walk of Fame instead of a star.

1846. More tigers exist in captivity in Texas than in the wild worldwide.

1847. There are no cats in Alberta, Canada.

1848. Eating snow can be harmful because it attracts car exhaust fumes like a magnet.

1849. According to a DNA study of dogs, the Chow Chow and the Shiba Inu are the most closely related to wolves.

1850. Inuits, Native Americans, and select Siberians have a gene that is linked to cold tolerance.

1851. On December 19th, 2016, the city of Chicago was colder (-30 F) than the surface of Mars (-2 F).

1852. A politc person is more likely to betray you in the future especially if that person wasn't polite to you in the past.

1853. The first international phone call was made on Christmas Day in 1900 when John W. Atkins called to Cuba. After a long silence, Cuba's response was, "I don't understand you."

1854. German troops used tablets of crystal meth to keep them awake for 3 days and three nights during the invasion of France in World War II.

1855. Originally water melons were harvested in Africa for their water content. Back then they had a nasty, bitter flavor, but centuries of selective breeding made them extra tasty.

1856. About 10 percent of Europeans are immune to HIV because they have an ancestor who survived bubonic plague.

1857. A water treatment plant was home to 107 million spiders.

1858. The first carrots were purple in color.

1859. Yawning and stretching at the same time is called pandiculating.

1860. There is an inconsistency with the US constitution where US could become a dictatorship despite its individual articles to protect democracy. It was discovered by a mathematician Kurt Godel while preparing for his US citizenship exam.

1861. Cigarette butts are the most littered item in the world, with an estimated 4.5 trillion littered annually. Each butt can take 5 to 400 years to completely break down.

1862. According to a Chinese tradition, eating chicken at a person's funeral helps the departed soul fly to heaven.

1863. 18 new viruses were discovered by scientists by sampling 133 New York City rats.

1864. The Aztecs imposed penalties like head-shaving, property destruction, and death upon people who were repeatedly found to be drunk.

1865. In 1984 Presidential Election, Ronald Reagan was 3,761 votes shy in Minnesota of winning every state.

1866. Most of the gift givers think that cash will be the least appreciated gift, when it is the most appreciated.

1867. The only person to ever win Nobel prizes in different areas of science is Marie Curie.

1868. In 1788 in the Battle of Karansebes the Austrian Army attacked itself resulting in 10,000 deaths.

1869. One of the Olympic Silver winners in Javelin throwing was Julius Yego who learned it by watching YouTube videos.

Thank you for reading Random Facts. If you enjoyed this book, please leave a review on Amazon.

Printed in Great Britain
by Amazon

50209725R00106